DYING FOR CHANGE

"Leith Anderson is astute biblically and sociologically. He has read deeply and thought profoundly about leadership and the styles that are mandated in a variety of contexts. . . . The book is strong descriptively and prescriptively."

WARREN S. BENSON
Vice President of Professional Doctoral Programs, Trinity Evangelical Divinity School

". . . in a very sensitive and well-balanced way he has given the formula and guidelines for maintaining the delicate tension between revelation and relevance . . . 'must' reading for all who desire stability in light of required change and transition."

DR. THOMAS F. ZIMMERMAN
Former General Superintendent, The General Council of the Assemblies of God

"If only such a book had been available when I finished seminary. . . . Understanding more clearly the need for change and how to accomplish it would undoubtedly have made my three pastorates more successful."

ROBERT P. DUGAN, JR.
Director, National Association of Evangelicals

"Leith Anderson writes as a successful practitioner . . . shows how a church, instead of dying, can experience a remarkable infusion of revitalizing vision and thus become relevantly effective."

VERNON C. GROUNDS
President Emeritus, Professor of Counseling and Ethics, Conservative Baptist Seminary

"A superb book on the critical issues facing every church and para-church organization . . . describes the reality of today and tells you how to shape the world of tomorrow."

LYLE E. SCHALLER
Yokefellow Institute

"Valuable insight for every pastor and church in the task of being Christ's church in this day at their location."

WIN ARN
President, Church Growth

DYING FOR CHANGE

LEITH ANDERSON

BETHANY HOUSE PUBLISHERS
MINNEAPOLIS, MINNESOTA 55438

Manuscript edited by Judith Markham.

Published by Bethany House Publishers
A Ministry of Bethany Fellowship, Inc.
6820 Auto Club Road, Minneapolis, Minnesota 55438

Printed in the United States of America

Library of Congress Cataloging-in-Publication Data

Anderson, Leith, 1944–
    Dying for change / Leith Anderson.
        p.   cm.

    1. Christianity—United States.
    2. Religion and sociology—United States.
    3. United States—Social conditions—1980–
    4. United States—Church history—20th century.
    5. Change—Religious aspects—Christianity.
        I. Title.
BR526.A53   1990
277.3'0829—dc20   90–38750
ISBN 1–55661–107–2   CIP

To

Charles W. Anderson
Margery F. Anderson

. . . my parents
. . . givers of roots
. . . teachers of change

Leith Anderson is the senior pastor of Wooddale Church in Eden Prairie, Minnesota. He is a graduate of Moody Bible Institute, Bradley University (B.A.), Denver Seminary (M.Div.), and Fuller Theological Seminary (D.Min.). The author of two other books, he has served as seminary teacher, conference speaker, missions leader and as a member on numerous boards. He and his family make their home in Edina, Minnesota.

Contents

Introduction

THE CHURCH was desperate. Years of decline had taken a painful toll. "What we need," they said, "is a dynamic new pastor."

A blue-ribbon search committee did everything right to find the perfect leader. He was young but experienced, serious but witty, articulate but not intimidating, spiritual but worldly-wise. If anyone could turn this problem-ridden congregation around, he was the man.

When the pastoral candidate first addressed the congregation, he gave an inspiring description of his qualifications, experience, vision, and plans. His final line summed up his stirring presentation: "With God's help, I intend to lead this church forward into the nineteenth century!"

Surprised and embarrassed by the candidate's apparent mistake, the chairman of the search committee whispered loudly, "You mean 'the twentieth century!' "

To which the candidate replied, "We're going to take this one century at a time!"

Like the church in our "brand X" illustration, an estimated

85% of America's Protestant churches are either stagnating or dying. Many of the sincere and committed Christians who still faithfully fill the family pews in these churches hold on to the nostalgic hope that tomorrow will be yesterday. Others desperately want their churches to catch up with the times and meet the challenges of the present generation, but they don't know how. And still others doggedly fight the inevitable changes for the sake of traditions that would be better abandoned.

Parallel to the churches of America are a large number of para-church organizations that were born and blossomed with the post-World War II "baby boom." But like baby boomers, these organizations are starting to show signs of aging. Many of the founders are gone; many will go within the next decade or two. And the current generation of leaders, who often seem to lack the vision of the founders, are accused of merely managing others' dreams.

What is happening in our churches and our organizations? And what can we do about it? Many good people desperately want to know.

What is happening?

Change. Extraordinarily difficult but absolutely necessary change.

Change is an unavoidable part of life. Without change, life would soon become intolerably dull. We welcome the different seasons, variety in foods, new experiences, and the coming true of dreams. When the status quo becomes intolerable, we do everything we can to initiate change.

At the same time, we hate the changes brought about by deteriorating health, social upheaval, and intrusions into our comfort zones. Sometimes we react so strongly against the changes we dislike that we either try to ignore them or use all our resources to reverse them.

Change would be challenging enough if each person were an isolated island unconnected to anyone else. Life becomes enormously more complicated by the fact that everyone and everything is changing at the same time.

What happens to individuals and families also happens to groups of individuals. Schools, churches, businesses, organizations, and communities are composed of changing individuals, but they also have a changing corporate character of their own. The group certainly changes as a result of the members, but the corporate character can also control changes in the individuals.

All of this is to say that we cannot do our changing alone or assume that others will wait for us to catch up. Everyone is in motion. Each church member is changing while the church is changing while the society is changing. Change is not the choice. How we handle it is.

At the end of the twentieth century, the currents of society are becoming more powerful and the waves of change are crashing closer. It is increasingly difficult for any individual, family, business, organization, church, or community to escape the sweeping changes brought about by drugs, globalization, environmental pollution, political polarization, or economic realignments.

No one is isolated. No one is exempt. Whether for good or ill, whether we like it or not, change is inevitable.

But where is God in all this? you may ask. The Bible teaches that He is unchanging. He is the same yesterday, today, and forever. Yet if everything is changing, does God change also?

Two theological truths explain God's relationship to change: immutability and sovereignty.

Immutability is changelessness. God is infinitely above and beyond our finite, human changes. His character and attributes are set. His standards are absolute. He is the one fixed point in our fast-moving drama of life.

However, God is also sovereign. He orders and accomplishes His will in human affairs. He is deeply involved in our lives and circumstances.

If it were not for God, I think I would despair in this fast-changing world of ours. I would be tempted to think that life is like a roulette game where every outcome is a matter of chance, and the odds against winning are enormous. Instead, I believe that God works in and through change to accomplish

His purposes. What seems silly or senseless to me fits perfectly into His plan.

Only this confidence in God's stability and involvement allows me to walk confidently and expectantly through this world of inevitable change.

Chapter 1

Now and Then

"THIS IS NOT your father's Oldsmobile" sings the advertising jingle, attempting to attract younger buyers for the troubled General Motors division. Actually, my father did drive Oldsmobiles, and I thought they were great cars. I especially remember his blue 1954 convertible—beautiful, powerful, and classy. I'd like to own that car today. But I wouldn't want it for everyday driving—just as a collector's item to show off in the summertime and to bring back pleasant childhood memories.

Not that there's anything wrong with a 1954 Olds. It's just not a car for the 1990s. It had no seat belts, no air conditioning, no cassette deck, no radial tires, no pollution control equipment, and no cruise control. What was state-of-the-art in automotive technology and design forty years ago is now barely acceptable for basic transportation.

In 1954 my father not only drove a great car, he also pastored a great church. He was there for more than three decades and his ministry was state-of-the-art. I remember when Sunday school attendance reached 1,000, making Brookdale Baptist

Church in suburban New York City one of America's larger Protestant churches. Those were the days when Sunday school attendance exceeded worship service attendance and when single morning services were the norm. My father insisted that a second morning service not be added lest the church's unity somehow be threatened.

Services lasted ninety minutes, and the sermon filled most of that time. Since altar calls were the primary means of evangelism, almost every service concluded with an "invitation to come forward." The Sunday evening service was often as well-attended as the morning service, and there was usually a large turnout for Wednesday night prayer meeting. New people were reached through home visitation, Sunday school attendance contests, summertime tent meetings, and regular radio programs. Those were "the good old days," and I remember them fondly and with gratitude.

Like my father, I pastor a suburban church. But a lot has changed in the intervening four decades. Today largeness is not a thousand, but thousands. Wooddale Church in suburban Minneapolis has thirteen pastors along with a support staff made up of secretaries, custodians, musicians, interns, bookkeeper, food service director, preschool staff, and program para-professionals. Sunday services last sixty minutes, including a twenty-seven-minute sermon. Multiple Sunday schools and worship services are not only necessary, but highly desirable. While crowded out on Sunday mornings, our Sunday evening service is only occasionally full. In fact, our church is unusual in that we even have a Sunday evening service. Altar calls are not part of our evangelistic strategy. People are reached through small groups, discovery classes, affinity evangelism, counseling, and a variety of constantly changing approaches. Sunday school contests don't work, home visitation is often unwelcome, and religious radio reaches only the already religious.

My father and I share many common bonds, but our churches are as different as our cars. Between then and now, both the world and the church have changed dramatically.

The Culture, the Christian, and the Church

Every Sunday morning when I stand in the pulpit to preach a sermon, I face an enormous challenge. I come as an individual Christian with a deep personal commitment to Jesus Christ as my Savior and Lord. I come as a pastor who loves the church and the people of the church. I come as an American born in the 1940s and living in the 1990s.

My task is to take the Bible and make it relevant to those who listen. Yet the Bible was written not only in languages different from ours but in totally different cultures and centuries. Translating it into English may be the easiest part; translating it into twentieth-century American culture is far more difficult. So I must operate from several presuppositions.

1. *God's truth is transcendent.* In other words, the Bible's revelation is for every culture, language, and generation. The Bible gives God's truth in a cultural container. The truth is absolute; the container is relative. We must pour the truth out of the container of first century Hebrew-Greek culture and into the container of twentieth-century American culture. When done properly, not a drop of truth is lost.

A simple example is 1 Corinthians 16:20, which says, "Greet one another with a holy kiss." The truth resident here is that Christians should give warm, kind greetings to each other as an expression of their spiritual solidarity. In Corinth they kissed each other. In Minneapolis we shake hands or hug each other.

2. *The church is the body of Christ.* That's what it says in Ephesians 4 and 5. At first this sounds strange to modern Americans, who often have difficulty with metaphors anyway.

What we must do is think in terms of Jesus having two bodies. Body #1 was a physical body, born of the Virgin Mary on the first Christmas. That body became the vehicle for God's Word and work in the first century—all the gifts, all the miracles, all the representation of God. When Body #1 ascended to heaven, Body #2 came into being.

Body #2 was born at Pentecost in Jerusalem and was called the "church" (Acts 1). The word itself has multiple meanings,

including "called out ones" and "assembly." The description
of the growth and further development of Body #2 is found
throughout the rest of the New Testament. The church is people who belong to Jesus Christ, assemble together, have spiritual gifts, and carry out God's Word and work in every suc-
cessive century.

Sometimes the New Testament refers to the church as all
Christians everywhere. Theologians have called this the church
universal. However, the vast majority of times the New Testament refers to the church as a local group of believers in a
specific place (such as Corinth, Ephesus, Thessalonica, or Jerusalem) at a specific time. Most of us have minimal compre-
hension of the universal church because it is so large, broad,
and widely distributed. Our experience is confined to the local
churches we belong to or observe.

This does not mean that any group of Christians automatically makes a church. That is a popular misconception. To be
a church, a group must meet certain conditions, including doctrine, fellowship, communion, and prayer (Acts 2:42). The
most visible condition is one of organization, including the
offices of elder (bishop) and deacon (1 Tim. 3).

Often I have heard people say, "The church isn't an or-
ganization; it's an organism." That is a misleading half-truth.
Yes, the church is an organism in the sense that all parts are
interdependent and connected to Jesus Christ as the Head (1
Cor. 12). But show me any organism that is not organized!
Even a paramecium is organized. In fact, much of the New
Testament addresses the organizational life of local first-
century churches.

In the twentieth century we coined the word "para-church"
to describe a body related to the church but not actually the
church. Para-church refers to religious organizations that do
church work but are not organized to be churches.

Actually, para-church organizations have been in existence
almost since the beginning of the church. These include religious orders, missionary societies, colleges, and evangelistic
groups. Generally, these groups seek to operate by the same
New Testament principles as the local church, although they

often are more open to adopting the organizing structures of secular institutions, businesses, and universities. Most para-church organizations say they are extensions of the church and subject to the church, but in reality that is seldom true.

Because of their close relationship, frequent overlap, and parallel purposes, however, the church and the para-church may be addressed together in terms of trends in the world and in our country.

3. *Knowing the Bible is not enough.* The church has a responsibility to understand people and the culture in which they live. This means that the Bible must be made relevant to today's culture in order to benefit today's people.

Life is difficult and disappointing, and typical churchgoers are struggling to survive. They come to church overflowing with needs—family, marriage, job, money, health, relationships—and looking for answers. They need hope and meaning and have turned to the church because they can't find it elsewhere.

Frankly, evangelical Christianity has done well on revelation (the Bible) but poorly on relevance (the culture). This phenomenon may be partially explained by the static nature of Scripture and the dynamic nature of society—that is, the Bible doesn't change but the culture does. This has been markedly evident over the past fifty years.

Putting It in Perspective

The last half of the twentieth century has been a transition time in history. We have moved out of a long era of comparative stability and predictability into a parenthesis of instability and unpredictability. Perhaps it is presumptuous to say this is a transition because it presupposes a lengthy future era when history will be more stable and events more predictable, and there is no way we can know that. Our best guess is based on review of earlier epochs, intervening transitions, and new epochs that have followed—the cycle of history. What we can say from experience is that the half century from 1950 to 2000 has been a period of breathtaking changes and extraordinary volatility.

Compare our generation to the Hebrew generation one thousand years before Christ. That was a time of transition too. King Saul was on his way out and King David was on his way in, marking the beginning of the long Davidic dynasty that would rule Israel for nearly five hundred years. But the changeover was painful. Their world was at war. On the home front there was civil war between those loyal to David and those following the army of Saul. On an international scale, they were battling the neighboring nation of Philistia. First Chronicles 12 lists those who deserted Saul and joined David in order to effect the dynastic change. This includes the "men of Issachar, who understood the times and knew what Israel should do" (12:32). There were only two hundred of them out of a population of millions, but at least they were attempting to understand what was happening and make a difference.

Today, there are modern men and women of Issachar. They are the ones who try to understand what is happening in order to decide what should be done. They are the ones who look at both the past and the present to determine action for the future.

The danger lies in thinking we can predict the future from the past. For example, in 1950 *Fortune* magazine asked eleven distinguished Americans to predict what life would be like in 1980. In those days the United States enjoyed a trade surplus of $3,000,000,000, so no one predicted a trade deficit thirty years later. David Sarnoff, chairman of RCA, was sure that by 1980 ships, airplanes, locomotives, and even individual automobiles would be atomically fueled. He said that homes would have atomic generators and that guided missiles would transport mail and other freight over great distances. Henry R. Luce, editor in chief of *Time* magazine, predicted the end of poverty by 1980. Mathematician John von Neumann expected energy to be free thirty years later.

The prognosticators were all wrong. They assumed the future would be like the present, only more so. In 1950 this country stood on the threshold of a new era of technology and a booming period of economic prosperity; we believed things would only get better and better. We could not foresee the energy crisis of 1973, the war in Vietnam, or the multitude of other unpredictable events that would occur between 1950 and 1980.

All of this means that we must always strike a balance between risk and reason. We must take the risk of anticipating the future by understanding the times, but we must also avoid the unfounded assumption that tomorrow will be like today.

With this in mind, let's examine recent changes in our world and country and use them as a basis for looking to the future.

Chapter 2

Present and Predictable Changes

DURING MAY 1990, I visited the People's Republic of China. I had thought of this nation with more than a billion people as backward and isolated, but I learned how interconnected our world really is. We flew into Beijing on a brand-new Boeing 747 made in America; we flew out of Beijing on an equally new Soviet tri-jet. In Xian they told me that Adidas sneakers are "out" this year but Reeboks are in. And in Guangzhou they keep up with current events by watching Dan Rather and the CBS Evening News broadcast from Hong Kong.

The World

Globalization began with the European colonization of the Western Hemisphere and Africa. Stories of distant cultures and products from different countries forced changes everywhere, but provincialism was strong and the process was slow.

With World War II, the speed of globalization accelerated. Unprecedented numbers of American GIs had seen foreign countries. This exposure led to international business and in-

ternational missions, and the emerging age of modern technology and global communications expanded. Space satellites
made instant telephone calls and television reports an everyday
experience. Jet planes shrunk travel time and cost to a fraction
of what it had been a hundred years earlier. These phenomena
increasingly fed on each other until today no culture can remain
isolated.

Western Europe is implementing a common currency tran-
scending national economies. The long-stemmed candy roses
sold in Rome are manufactured by Joanne Henry of Candy
Flowers, Inc. in Mentor, Ohio. Thirty-nine percent of the parts
Americans use in manufacturing currently come from other
countries. IBM imports 37% of the parts it uses in production.
Japan imports raw materials from the United States for its steel
industry and oil from Iran to fuel its engines. The Australian
stock market is directly affected by the rise or fall of the Dow
Jones Average on Wall Street, which is affected by the changing
value of the dollar in London and Frankfurt. Acid rain from
pollution in North America causes deterioration of ancient
buildings in Italy, while destruction of the rain forest in Brazil
contributes to the depletion of the ozone layer over Antarctica.

As a result, says *The Futurist* magazine, "Nationalistic self-
interest will continue to yield to international trade cooperation. Both developing and developed countries will focus less
on dominating economic competitors and, instead, will put
efforts into liberalizing trade cooperation."[1]

This is a shocking change for Americans who are used to
calling the shots, dominating the world, and setting the terms
of international cooperation. For decades we have lived with a
real or perceived sense of international superiority, but it appears those days are over. If we are to survive, we must co-
operate and submit. Such an adjustment may be easier in economics than in lifestyle, where we will have to learn to get
along with other races, other languages, other cultural practices, and other religions.

Nowhere has the effect of globalization been felt more rad-

[1]Marvin J. Cetron, Wanda Rocha, and Rebecca Luckins, "Into the 21st Century:
Long-Term Trends Affecting the United States"; THE FUTURIST (July-August,
1988), 31.

ically than in the church in North America. During the past twenty-five years, the numerical center of Christianity has shifted southward and eastward, so that the West is no longer the center of Christian faith. Africa, which at the beginning of the twentieth century was a focal point for much missionary endeavor, may well be a Christian continent by the end of the century, at least south of the Sahara Desert. In the Philippines the Protestant church is growing at 10% per year. The goal of 50,000 churches by A.D. 2000 is on target, building off a base of only 3,400 churches in 1974. Global Mapping Project in Pasadena, California, estimates that China may have 20 to 25% of the world's evangelicals. Costa Rica's evangelical churches grew 100% in four years, and Brazil has 24,000,000 evangelicals—more than all of Europe, outside the Soviet Union.

Parallel to globalization has come *urbanization*. Enormous population shifts have moved millions of people out of rural areas and into the cities of the world. Mexico City, Tokyo, and Sao Paulo are becoming super cities, where space and services cannot keep up with the expanding population. This phenomenon is hard to explain since it is so widespread. It is difficult to find corresponding reasons why populations from rural America and rural Brazil and rural Japan would migrate to the cities.

The corresponding challenges are frightening. In Third World countries expanding poverty and deep disappointment from unmet expectations feed political unrest. While the countryside empties, the cities bloat, creating an atmosphere ripe for explosion in countries where governments are unstable and corrupt and where economies are often at or near bankruptcy.

In rural areas people deal with life on a smaller scale. In the city the public school may have thousands, and the hospital has more beds than the small town has people. In rural areas the extended family is often close. When part of the family moves to the city, those relationships are distanced, if not broken. It contributes to the disintegration of traditions and the acceptance of change.

The pressure for change is much greater in urban areas because the options are greater. A daughter may enter prostitution or a son may join a street gang. On the positive side, the family that relocates to a city may be more likely to become Christian than the family that stays within the confined pagan structures of a rural village.

In "The Sixty Mile City," Lyle Schaller discusses the effect of these differences in America. He observes that many rural churches are composed of older people born before 1940 with fewer than 100 in regular attendance. The pastor is often younger and inexperienced, and the church is more likely to belong to an old-line denomination. By contrast, the churches in urban areas are more likely to have a younger congregation, have more than 200 in attendance, be denominationally independent, and be led by an older, experienced pastor.[2]

Meanwhile, on a global scale, missiologists are scrambling to catch up on methodology. For the past two hundred years, Christian missions have targeted rural areas rather than cities. Experiences and strategies are out-of-date, and personnel and resources need to be urbanized. All of this is taking place at a time when the countries that have traditionally sent missionaries are experiencing stable or declining populations, fewer missionary volunteers, and increasingly limited access to many of the countries with the largest urban populations.

One of the most surprising changes at the close of the twentieth century is worldwide *democratization*. The year 1989 saw sweeping political changes from China to Europe. The yearning for freedom from tyranny is nothing new. What is amazing is the kind of simultaneous uprisings, apparently unconnected, that took place in the cities and smaller towns of East Germany and Romania. If there is a connection between the cry for democracy and the collapse of Communism across borders and cultures, it is hard to find. The best guess is that worldwide democratization has been both promoted and made possible by aspects of globalization such as communication. While it was possible to control most of the information people received in 1950, it became impossible by 1989.

An interesting wrinkle in all this is that with democracy

---

[2]Lyle Schaller, "The Transformation of Rural America and the Emergence of the Sixty-Mile City," *Net Results*, August 1988, 5–7.

comes nationalism, which in many ways is the opposite of globalization. Small countries like Lithuania and Estonia had their national identity swept away in the formation of the USSR. Now these people, and others around the world, are seeking personal identity by returning to their own national identity and the language and culture of their ancestors.

There is a positive side to nationalism as people attempt to define their difference in an increasingly homogeneous world. While the rest of the world seems to be merging together, the nationalists take a healthy pride in race, art, dance, music, patriotism, and tradition.

However, nationalism also breeds exclusivism where minorities become the targets of discrimination. The globalization that brings Turks into Europe as laborers also makes it possible for them to be viewed as unwelcome foreigners. Like many changes in our world, nationalism is a reality with which we must cope whether we agree or disagree with its consequences.

Related to nationalism and the search for identity is the worldwide resurgence of *fundamentalism*. This is best illustrated by the enormous religious and social changes in Iran under the late Ayatollah Khomeni. For an entire generation the Shah of Iran worked to develop a modern and largely secular nation. Iran became a close ally of the United States, and the culture was increasingly influenced by Western values, dress, and thought. Then came the Islamic Revolution. Western ties were broken, and Koranic law was imposed. Women educated at American universities were forced to cover their faces and wear black from head to toe. Capital punishment became an everyday occurrence. Imams (religious leaders) dominated the political arena.

Such fundamentalism is not just an Iranian or an Islamic phenomenon. A resurgence of fundamental religious and cultural values is also evident in India's Hinduism and America's Christianity. It is all part of the modern search for roots and identity in old traditions and beliefs that run counter to the tidal wave of secular technology and globalization.

In earlier generations it was easier to remain isolated from global changes. Local cultures and economies were stronger and more protective. Today, even the hermit who hides in a cave or the monk who meditates in a monastery is not immune from satellites, acid rain, and international products at the local marketplace.

The Country

Changes in America cannot be isolated from changes throughout the rest of the world. Nonetheless, we do have our own national expression of global changes and our own distinct trends. Basically these fall into ten categories.

1. *Mobility*

My mother was born in northern England and emigrated to the United States as an adult. My father, the grandson of Swedish immigrants, was born and raised in Camden, New Jersey. While my wife Charleen and I grew up in neighboring towns in New Jersey, we went away to college in Illinois and have not lived within a thousand miles of our immediate families since. We have extended family in Florida, California, Pennsylvania, and Texas. Some of our friends have changed addresses so many times that our address book doesn't have room for another listing.

Such mobility is nothing new. Since the days of the wagon train, we Americans have moved freely from place to place. The rate of mobility increased significantly after World War II, however, largely because of returning GIs who were used to moving and the rapid expansion of the economy under peace and prosperity. With increased urbanization, there is every reason to expect increased mobility.

Vance Packard became the first national chronicler of the downside of mobility in his best-selling book *A Nation of Strangers*, showing how the mobility that gives freedom, socioeconomic rise, and social excitement can also severely damage social structures and traditional values. When parents, grandparents, and grandchildren are thousands of miles apart, extended families no longer share child-rearing responsibilities.

Traditional values that were reinforced in small towns and established neighborhoods often dissipate in a community of newcomers and strangers.

Combined with urbanization, mobility often results in less family time and community involvement. Commuting time can add up to hours a day. There are few hours left to spend with children, be a community volunteer, or get to know the neighbors around the block. Motor vehicles are no longer just transportation; they are "living rooms on wheels," with climate control, high-quality sound equipment, phones, adjustable seating, and eating spaces. One recent mini-van model boasted fourteen cupholders for a vehicle seating eight people. McDonald's, Burger King, Wendy's, and Hardees often do more business at the drive-through than at the inside counter. The car has become the living room, the sound studio, the office, and the dining room for many modern mobile families.

While mobility is mostly a matter of physical relocation, it is also a mentality. Movement in society creates an openness to mobility within institutional and personal relationships. Just as we may move from city to city or house to house, we may also move from marriage to marriage and job to job. This mobility has significantly altered the way many Americans view the church.

Once upon a time churches were seen as destinations. When you found the church you wanted to join, you stayed with it through good and bad times. With the present mobility mentality, churchgoers now see specific churches as "way stations" along the journey of life. They may join one church for a certain chapter of their lives but have no difficulty moving along to the next church (at the next way station) when the next chapter begins. Even people who continue to live in the same city may change addresses, jobs, and churches every three to five years. This can be particularly confusing and painful for the pastor from an older generation who sees this as a personal rejection of his ministry.

2. Coloring

Take a look at the population changes experienced and predicted in the U.S. between 1980 and 2000. In 1980 there were

14.6 million Hispanics; by 1995 they will total 26.8 million. The 26.5 million black Americans will grow to 35.8 million by 2000. Those of Asian descent increased from 3.5 million to 5.1 million between 1960 and 1985 (almost 50%). By 2000, the total could be 10 million. At the same time, the Anglo population is static or slightly declining. Persons once referred to as "minorities" are increasingly designated "persons of color," referring to Blacks, Hispanics, Asians, Native Americans, and other "non-whites."

This coloring of America is a result of both immigration and high birth rate, and the impact is greater in some parts of the country than others. California, for example, projects that whites will be a minority by the year 2000.

The enormous tension facing our society in general and our churches in particular is how to justly assimilate persons of color and still encourage ethnic identity. The white population is aging. Also, whites have traditionally considered minorities a threat rather than an opportunity, both in the community and in the church.

Recognizing this challenge, black theologian and sociologist James Earl Massey writes:

> Quite contrary to the concern in the late 1950s and early 1960s to blend us all into the larger cauldron of American stew, the succeeding decades have underscored the point that a true democracy does *not* demand absorption of differences and distinctives. Ethnic strengths need not be disruptive if group autonomy, proportional representation, and equality within the national system are honored and guaranteed.[3]

3. Graying

For the first time in our history, there are more Americans over 65 than there are teenagers. The over–65 senior citizen group has increased 50% since 1950, and it will increase an-

---

[3]"The Coloring of America," *Christianity Today Institute:* "Into the Next Century: Trends Facing the Church" (January 17, 1986), 10-I.

other 75% over the next four decades as baby boomers move into retirement.

At the same time, the youth population is shrinking. During the 1990s the 18–25 age group will decrease by 12%. In 1980 there were 4.2 million 19 year olds; in 1992 there will be 3.1 million. The fastest-growing age group in America is the age group over 85. By 1998 the number of Americans over 85 will have grown by 50%. At the same time there will be a 45% increase in 45–50 year olds and a 21% increase in those 75–84. In 1985 there were 6 million over 80, but by the year 2000 there will be 10 million.

These older Americans also hold increased economic and political power. Today's elderly have 13% more per capita income than the rest of the population, and the majority of the wealth of America is controlled by persons over age 50. That percentage of wealth control will significantly increase as baby boomers increase income and savings while they age in the life cycle.

The elderly vote more and move less, resulting in disproportionate political clout. Public policy is already responding to their interests and will increasingly do so. We are already seeing government move wealth and services from the young to the old. Government spending for the present generation is being funded by debt to be paid by future generations of workers. Less money is being spent on schools for the young, and more money is being spent on health care and nursing homes for the elderly. Wages for new employees are often stalled by the cost of expensive early retirements of older employees.

While the standard retirement age is still 65, many people are retiring earlier. One quarter of the men aged 55–59 now identify themselves as retired.

It is estimated that by the year 2050, 41% of all compensation paid in the U.S. will go for Social Security payments. In 2020 the peak of the baby boom generation will move into retirement, and for every retiree receiving benefits there will be only two workers paying into the Social Security system. That compares to 3.3 workers per retiree in 1989. To prepare for this enormous cost Congress has regularly increased the

Social Security tax, until many lower-level workers are paying more in Social Security taxes than in income taxes. The scenario for the immediate future is one of growing power and influence for the elderly and growing poverty and powerlessness for the young. Older voters will elect politicians who will enact laws favoring senior citizens. Older workers will have disproportionate influence in their companies. Older leaders will tend to dominate churches and other voluntary organizations.

The graying of the population will certainly affect religious institutions. Organizations focused on youth may be replaced by those focused on age, and aging donors will become the primary financial support base.

4. Women

Women have always worked. Prior to World War II, when America was a more agricultural economy, most worked at home or on the family farm. During the war women entered the commercial work force in increased numbers to alleviate the domestic manpower shortage. After the war, what had begun as a military and industrial necessity for the nation became an economic necessity for the American family.

Today 55% of American women work outside the home, and the Labor Department estimates that the figure will rise to 61%. While many are employed out of economic necessity, many equally see this as the pursuit of a career. Women comprise 20% of America's physicians, twice the proportion of 1970, and one third of the current medical school students are women. Increasingly, women are entering, if not leading, fields traditionally dominated by men.

More and more women are less likely to leave the work force during childbearing years. In 1987, for the first time, over half of the new mothers went back to work within a year of giving birth, compared to 31% in 1976.

This change in American society has had and will continue to exert great influence on the church and para-church organizations. In the past women have been the bulk of volunteers for churches, school activities, and community services. This is no longer possible. Women who work are not available during the day, and when they come home they are occupied with traditional household responsibilities. Many are also single mothers who may themselves be in great need of those services conducted by volunteers. What some older church leaders perceive as declining volunteerism because of lower commitment levels is often lower volunteerism because of increased commitments elsewhere.

As women assume greater leadership and latitude in the workplace, they will expect greater access to traditionally male positions in the church. This clashes with the teaching of the Roman Catholic Church and many conservative Protestants. Thus, there is the potential for alienation and polarization. Some women (and men who support their expanded role in religion) will be so alienated that they will drop out. The equally great danger is that churches and denominations will polarize into opposing camps over the appropriate role of women in the church.

5. *Pluralism*

Just a generation ago there were only three television networks, three major automobile manufacturers, few medical specialists, identical interest rates at all banks, and the same fares on every airline. Magazine racks at the corner drugstore carried a limited selection of periodicals such as *Time, Life, Look,* and *The Saturday Evening Post.*

Today the choices are mind-boggling. Airline fares change thousands of times every month as computer programs constantly adjust to fares posted by competing carriers. Every bank has a different interest rate depending on the amount of deposit and term of investment. Magazines are highly specialized, with separate publications for everything from computers (specialized by type), to skiing (downhill and cross country), to soap operas. Televisions come with 110 channel capacity and many parts of the country have cable choices ranging from sports to pornography, from English to Spanish, from opera to rock music, from 24-hour weather reports to 24-hour news channels.

Choices even extend into the area of religion. While multiple denominations and religious freedom have been the backbone of America since its beginning, northern European Protestantism dominated American culture until 1960. Protestant values entered the schoolroom with the *McGuffey Reader* and the Lord's Prayer. Controversy rolled across America in the 1960s when Roman Catholic John Kennedy ran for the presidency. A key campaign issue revolved around the Pope's potential influence over the would-be president.

While many vestiges of the Protestant ethic remain, other alternatives have greatly increased. Secularism has won numerous battles to replace Christian values in the schools and other public institutions. New Age religious notions have popularized belief in reincarnation and other non-Christian doctrines that were seldom heard a generation ago. There has been a switch from absolute values to relative values. Many Americans have no clear conviction of what is right and what is wrong; instead they hold to a philosophy of "what's right or wrong for me is different from what's right or wrong for you." This is the ultimate expression of American individualism and independence.

Relativism poses a series of threats and problems for Christians. On the one hand, Christians have less common ground with unbelievers. It is harder to evangelize those who do not agree on basic issues such as the existence of God, the authority of the Bible, the wrongness of sin, and the need for forgiveness. On the other hand, the pluralism of our society has crept into many Christians' belief systems; they think it intolerant to condemn non-Christian belief as wrong. In fact, the fastest growing ethic among many evangelical Christians is universal acceptance and compassion, along with a heightened tolerance of relativism and diversity.

6. *Shifts in Segmentation*

During the first half of this century, industrialists and merchandisers introduced a system of economic segmentation that divided society into three classes: lower, middle, and upper. Further segmentation gradually subdivided each of these into three parts until we ended up with lower middle class, middle middle class and upper middle class. The most famous example of marketing to society's segments came from General Motors with its similar cars designed and priced for each segment. Lower to upper classes were sold a hierarchy of vehicles called Chevrolet, Pontiac, Oldsmobile, Buick, and Cadillac.

Churches have never been very comfortable with segmentation by class but have practiced segmentation by geography. Many denominations established geographical lines defining parishes, where everyone within a certain area was expected to worship at the church designated for that area. Churches were free to win converts within those boundaries, but not beyond. Missionaries practiced the same principle overseas by establishing "comity" arrangements determining which missions worked where.

Interestingly, geographical segmentation often resulted in the socioeconomic segmentation churches deliberately avoided. Many communities are single class and single race. Rich people live in certain towns and poor people live in other towns. Whites live in their neighborhoods and minorities live in their neighborhoods. Result? Churches that segment by geography end up being segmented economically and racially.

The last half of the twentieth century has seen segmentation become increasingly based on demographics and psychographics rather than geographics. Demographics divide people into groups by gender, age, race, education, income, marital status, ethnic origin, and other characteristics. Each of these groups may be determined to have characteristics and preferences distinct to themselves. For example, phone-answering machines are very popular among 18–29 year olds, with more than half saying such machines have made life better. By contrast, most older Americans don't have and usually don't like phone-answering machines. Many not only refuse to own them, they also refuse to use them, hanging up rather than listening to or talking to a tape.

Psychographics seeks to segment society by life orientation

or the choices people make. For example, some people are "survivors" and others are "achievers." Survivors shop for bargains and are motivated by surviving to the next day and year. Achievers are motivated by success. They shop for clothes, food, and cars that will impress others and give an appearance of success.

Segmentation is constantly changing. An example is marital status. In 1950 most people were either married or single. Single usually meant never married but could mean widowed or divorced. Marital status is still a popular and routine means for classifying people, and many churches still have adult Sunday school classes segmented on the basis of marital status. However, millions of Americans now claim that marital status is not an appropriate definition of who they are. Employers who inquire about marital status or use the information as a basis for employment violate anti-discrimination laws. Besides which, many couples are hard to classify: many live together and have children but are never legally married; others are legally married but do not live together; a few are legally divorced but still relate to each other as if they were married; and a growing number are in the process of getting a divorce but say they are single and act as if they are.

The high schools of America are probably the epitome of demographic and psychograpic segmentation. The movie *The Breakfast Club* is the story of five teenagers assigned to a Saturday detention class. They are all from different "tribes" in the school that usually have nothing to do with each other. Each tribe has its own rules, its own dress code, its own social code, and its own tables in the cafeteria. Typical tribes in many high schools include the jocks, the preppies, the druggies, the students, the nerds, and the normies. Church youth pastors who attempt to bring together twenty high schoolers from the same school, community, and church are often frustrated by the impossibility of group cohesiveness because the teens are all from different tribes and are virtually forbidden to cross the lines. It is societal segmentation to an extreme.

The segmenting of American society has great implications for the church. For instance, people are more and more likely to choose churches on the basis of demographics and psychographics rather than geography. They will drive past half a dozen churches and even into another town if that is where they feel comfortable and where their needs are met.

Some churches intentionally reach people by principles of segmentation while others continue to take a geographic approach. Sometimes both work. Sometimes both fail. What is most tragic is when a geographic approach to outreach does not fit the segment of people in the immediate community. This often results in a church filled with people who once lived in the area and have moved out, but who continue to drive back to attend church. They perpetuate an approach to ministry aimed at a community that no longer exists. The streets may have the same names and the houses have the same appearance, but the people living there are demographically and psychographically different.

7. Short-term Commitments

Modern American culture places great emphasis on self, independence, and personal fulfillment. Combined with mobility and uncertainty, these trends make long-term commitments seem inappropriate. This is a phenomenon that is having a major impact on our institutions.

When rapid change appears to be the norm, people are reluctant to commit to anything. Unlike the Japanese, who spend their entire lives working for one employer, most Americans change jobs several times. This may be out of economic necessity or for career advancement. Or it may be the result of mergers, corporate takeovers, or changing economics that reduce or remove an industry from the scene. A generation back corporate giants hired at good wages with great benefits. Now they are laying off and reducing benefits. Cheryl Russell, editor of *American Demographics* magazine, estimates that baby boomers will work at ten different jobs during their lifetime. On the average, workers now change careers three times in their lives.

Mobility has virtually removed the expectation of living a lifetime in the same house, and few homeowners pay off a thirty-year mortgage. Few expect to.

More marriages ended in divorce during the 1970s and 1980s than during any other period in American history. Not only has this stamped divorce as socially acceptable, it has also created a generation of children who have experienced divorce, single parent homes, and multiple marriages as the norm rather than the exception. While most couples entering marriage would say they are making a lifetime commitment, they know that divorce is a possibility if either or both are dissatisfied. This varies greatly from their grandparents' generation (and the laws of their grandparents' generation), which seldom saw divorce as an option. Marriage was perceived as permanent, no matter what.

Regardless of the "why" of short-term commitments, the frequency is easily observed. Fewer people are interested in joining clubs, taking on assignments, signing contracts, or doing anything that will reduce the options for future decisions.

As a result, church life and programs have been directly influenced. Sunday school teachers are much harder to recruit if a one-year, 52-Sunday commitment is required. Membership classes that used to last for weeks are now condensed into a single-day seminar. Short-term task force assignments are more popular than three-year board assignments. Sermons must stand alone rather than be connected in a several-week series, because more people attend church less frequently (so they can take weekend vacations, business trips, or participate in other activities). One-day seminars have replaced series and conferences that ran for seven consecutive days.

8. Decline in the Work Ethic

When a valve broke at one of the Coors factories in Golden, Colorado, most of the operation had to be shut down, causing enormous delays and lost revenue. Management called for an all-out effort to make the repairs and get the factory up and running again. Everyone responded and good progress was made—until the end of the second shift. At that point most of the younger workers punched out while many of the older workers expected to stay on the job until the work was done, even if it took all night. Two different generations were operating from two different work ethics: one saw work as time and money and the other saw it as a task to be accomplished.

Minnesota researcher and author Merton Strommen reports such changing attitudes among college students. Fifteen years ago, he says, the #1 goal of college freshman was "developing a meaningful philosophy of life"; today it has switched to "making money." The six million students now entering college show an increasing interest in material success and a declining interest in serving others, and those most motivated by making money has grown from 30% to 70%.

The Futurist magazine lists "decline in the work ethic" as one of the long-term trends affecting the United States:

> Tardiness is increasing, and sick-leave abuse is common. In contrast, two thirds of Americans would like to see an increase in the number of hours they work, rather than working shorter hours—if they were paid for those extra hours.
>
> Job security and high pay are not the motivators they once were, because there is a high degree of social mobility and because people now seek job fulfillment; in a poll, 48% of workers say they work because it "gives a feeling of real accomplishment."
>
> Fifty-five percent of the top executives interviewed in a recent poll say that erosion of the work ethic will have a major effect on corporate performance in the future.[4]

The Protestant work ethic is theologically rooted in the writings of John Calvin and sociologically described in the writings of Max Weber. For decades it was a strong motivating force in American culture as people sought to discover and live out their calling in life through their employment. Work in itself was considered good even if the task was menial. Meaning

---

[4]Marvin J. Cetron, Wanda Rocha, and Rebecca Luckins, "Into the 21st Century: Long-Term Trends Affecting the United States"; *THE FUTURIST* (July-August, 1988), 35–36.

to life was molded by doing one's job well and making a positive contribution to the community.

Now the focus has shifted to the remuneration for the work and the advantage to self. Accompanying this ethical shift is a major change in the availability of workers. When the baby boomers began to enter the work force in 1964 (at age 18), there was a flood of workers and a shortage of jobs. The surplus of available workers contributed to comparatively high national unemployment. For almost eighteen years the marketplace expanded to offset this, creating many new jobs. However, the sharp decline in the birthrate after 1964 resulted in a shortage of workers to fill this marketplace, which began to be felt in the 1980s. Consequently, the United States is now enjoying comparatively high employment but a growing shortage of workers.

During the 1980s, the fastest growing segment of the job market has been in the service industry where wages are relatively low. For those born after 1964, this computes out to a future with good employment prospects but lower earnings. Generally the flood of baby boomers has saturated the middle management market; now these same individuals are fiercely competing for a relatively small number of jobs in upper management.

9. Conservatism

Conservatism is a significant and surprising trend of the late twentieth century. In fact, many argue that Ronald Reagan did not conservatize America as much as a conservative America elected Ronald Reagan. And in many cases, younger Americans are more conservative than older Americans.

In 1975, 46% of people aged 20 to 29 (the oldest baby boomers) called themselves liberals . . . by 1985, only 29% of the 30-to-39-year-olds said they were liberals, a loss of 17 percentage points. Though the older baby boomers are still more likely to be liberal than older Americans, they are not as liberal as they used to be. They are even less liberal than people aged 30 to 39 were in 1975. Baby boomers in their 30s in 1985 are more likely to identify themselves as conservatives than as liberals—34% say they are conservatives, up from only 19% of 20-to-29-year-olds in 1975.[5]

People tend to be most conservative and cautious during their forties and fifties—the years when they are focused on family, children, jobs, houses, future retirement, and security. If recent developments are any indication, we can anticipate that the large population moving into their forties and fifties at the end of this century and the beginning of the next will be even more conservative.

Being politically conservative does not necessarily mean one is morally conservative, however. Many who vote for a politically conservative candidate hold liberal moral views on abortion, drugs, and sexual morality. This is directly related to the tolerance for pluralism, diversity, and even contradiction. Individualism allows for a collage of liberal and conservative views in the same person, which makes it very difficult, if not impossible, to accurately define what a conservative or a liberal currently is.

Another problem arises when some align religious, political, and cultural conservatism and attempt to lump them together. For example, a person may be religiously conservative in accepting the authority of the Bible, politically liberal in rejecting U.S. claims to the Panama Canal, and culturally undecided on the proper role of women in society.

Such diversity of views can cause great frustration within the church. Conservative churches struggle with members who believe their doctrinal creed but hold liberal views and practices on divorce and remarriage. Liberal churches may be equally uncomfortable with members who endorse the denomination's politically liberal position on South Africa's apartheid but brand the same church's stand on homosexual lifestyle as unbiblical and unacceptable.

---

[5]Cheryl Russell, *100 Predictions for the Baby Boom* (New York: Plenum Press, 1987), 175.

Most likely to benefit from conservative views is the structure and stability of the family. After many years of increase, we are finally seeing a decrease in the divorce rate. There were 22.6 divorces per 1,000 married women in 1980 but 21.7 divorces per 1,000 women in 1985. The institution of marriage is becoming more popular, as is having children. Fear of AIDS is at least one major factor promoting sexual monogamy and discouraging promiscuity. However, there may also be a growing desire for stable traditional families among those adults who have strong memories of parental divorce and growing up in stepfamilies.

10. *Cocooning*

This phenomenon recently observed by society watchers may be too new to label as a long-term trend, but it does fit with many of the other changes in America. Cocooning is the return to the home as the center of life's activities and relationships.

Executives at Domino's Pizza claim that their primary product is delivery not pizza. People are eating in instead of eating out. This trend promises a bright future for drive-through restaurants and food-delivery companies.

Large family rooms and kitchens have replaced the living room in the design of many new homes. Video tapes are one of America's booming industries, as friends and family gather around home entertainment centers to watch the latest movie release. Games like Trivial Pursuit and Pictionary are "bestsellers," requiring new editions and updates, and home exercise equipment is a popular alternative to joining a health club.

Along with these increased personal and family activities inside the home has come an equal aversion or resistance to strangers. Private security systems turn modern homes into fortresses secured against intruders. Door-to-door salespeople are not welcome, but highly specialized catalogues, direct-mail, cable TV home-shopping networks, and 800 numbers have become increasingly popular.

Again, these changes have had a strong impact on the

church. The traditional Sunday evening services of many evangelical churches have found themselves in direct competition with the American cultural conviction that Sunday night is "America's Night at Home." In fact, the church promoting Sunday night services may be perceived as opposing the very family life it officially endorses. And while door-to-door evangelism was once an effective means of bringing visitors to church and winning converts to Christ, that practice increasingly runs counter to the "unwelcome mat" Americans are putting out to strangers. Potential visitors are more likely to be attracted by direct-mail efforts, and evangelism is carried out more effectively through existing webs of relationships.

While many do not recognize it—or do not want to recognize it—there is no doubt that the sweeping changes in the world and the country are beginning to alter the face of religion.

Chapter 3

The Church Is Not an Island

I HAVE NEVER milked a cow. Only twice have I seen anyone else milk a cow—once on a grade school field trip when I was a boy and once at the Minnesota State Fair 4-H booth. But I'm not alone. Most Americans have never milked a cow. Yet many churches still hold their Sunday morning services at eleven o'clock, an hour originally chosen to accommodate the milking schedule of dairy farmers.

Churches that begin having earlier Sunday morning services are often surprised at the number of people who prefer to worship earlier so they can be home before noon to see the kickoff for the NFL football games. The shift away from farming and the popularity of football are examples of the changes that are affecting the times when Americans worship God.

Some may say that the sacred should not be subject to the secular, and often that is true (although there was certainly nothing sacred about milking cows or the hour chosen to accommodate that). However, we cannot view the church as an island isolated from the rest of society. It cannot be isolated. As the culture changes, the church changes.

Perhaps the greatest effect from outside the church is the growing influence of government involvement in America's churches. After two hundred years of independence and separation of church and state, government regulations and interventions are on the increase. This action is traceable to several specific incidents.

The PTL scandal involving Jim Bakker and his colleagues convinced the government and the public that large teleevangelism ministries needed some kind of outside regulation. While the religious community focused more on the moral issues in the case, it was the financial mismanagement that brought in the government. Because gifts are tax deductible, because such religious institutions are tax exempt, and because funds were used for personal benefit rather than for ministry, the federal government initiated court actions that closed down PTL and imprisoned its leader. This set a precedent for inquiries into other religious institutions, and we can expect the government to assume more and more responsibility for policing religion's finances.

The second significant case was the counseling malpractice lawsuit against the Grace Community Church of Sun Valley, California, when the parents of a counselee who committed suicide sued the church for damages, alleging that inappropriate pastoral counsel led to the suicide. The church has won repeated court cases, but once again a precedent has been set. The public and the courts now perceive that government may intervene and decide in matters of religious counsel. Clergy malpractice wasn't even in the vocabulary twenty-five years ago; now it is a very real threat, and many church institutional insurance policies routinely offer clergy malpractice coverage.

A third important precedent involves a series of conflicts related to religious differences that have ended up in the civil courts rather than being resolved within the religious community. These controversies range from parents who hire deprogrammers to rescue their children from cults, to Christian Science practitioners who deny their children medical care, to Seventh Day Adventists and other Sabbatarians who refuse to work on Saturday and protest employers who discriminate.

A fourth factor may prove to be the most significant of all. It is the growing number of municipalities that are attempting to limit church size through restrictive zoning ordinances. Many communities are saying "1,000 and no more." In all probability, this will become a church vs. state legal contest that will result in a landmark decision by the United States Supreme Court.

All of these conflicts called for resolution in the civil courts and have thus established a precedent for government involvement.

While there is little doubt that attempts to regulate religion will continue and even increase during the coming years, many wonder just *why* this has all come about. Is it Satan at work? Does it portend the end times? Or what?

No matter what your theological perspective on all this might be, the practical answer is that the differences between the secular and sacred are rapidly blurring in American society. For example, when the Constitution of the United States was drafted, the "spirit" of its citizens was considered the province of the church. People went to pastors for counseling, not to psychiatrists and psychologists. Today, thousands of men and women practice this discipline that is primarily defined as scientific rather than religious. Yet psychotherapists increasingly talk about the "spiritual" aspects of human life, while pastors increasingly use psychological terms and therapy. It is difficult to know where secular ends and sacred begins, and so it is left to the government to decide.

Or, consider the growing church involvement in day care centers, preschools, and parochial schools that are highly regulated and licensed by the state. Some churches refuse to submit to any government interference, while others want accreditation and credibility and seek to comply with all government regulations. The greatest conflicts arise when government values differ greatly from religious convictions. The state may decide that discrimination based on sexual preference or religious creed is illegal; but the church (or school or mission or para-church organization) firmly opposes homosexual practice on biblical grounds and insists that all employees agree to a

creed or statement of faith. As a result of these and other conflicts, we may expect increased litigation and more incidents of
civil disobedience.

Despite all this, the greatest social changes unique to the
church at the end of the twentieth century are coming from the
inside, not the outside.

Denominational Decline

At the end of 1989 the United Methodist Church, America's
second largest denomination, reported that its constituency had
dropped below nine million for the first time since it began to
keep records. In 1937 the Gallup Poll reported that 73% of
Americans were members of a church or synagogue. By 1988
this had dropped to 65%, the lowest ever. That was also the
year when, for the first time, Catholics were no more likely to
be church members than Protestants.

The past twenty-five years have been tough on denominations, especially mainline denominations and those outside the
South, where denominationalism is stronger. Equally serious
is the aging of those who are church members. Most denominations not only have a declining total number but an escalating
average age. Younger people just aren't joining denominational
churches.

One might expect that the decline of denominational membership would be paralleled by a decline in the national percentage of church attendance, but that is not the case. Approximately 40% of Americans say they go to church each
week, a percentage that has remained quite constant over recent decades. Equally interesting is the *increase* in religious
interest and conviction. In 1957, 69% of the population felt
religion had an increasing influence in their lives. That tumbled
to an all-time low of 14% in 1969 and 1970, and then shot back
up to 48% by 1985. In that same year almost all Americans
(95%) said they believed in God or a universal spirit, and 56%
of Americans said that religion was very important in their
lives.

In 1950, when many of the peaks were reached in the religious interest polls, membership in denominational churches was equated with religious beliefs. By 1990 that was no longer true. The fact that spiritual interest is rising while denominations decline indicates that the general population no longer sees a necessary connection between the two.

These are tough days for denominations as they lose people, power, and money. More important, they seem to be missing out on the spiritual vitality and renaissance in America. Let's consider why.

1. The great mobility of recent decades removed many people from their family roots, parents, and grandparents, as well as their hometown church and denomination. Often it was not possible to link up with the same denomination in their new location. This mobility, combined with a growing ecumenism that has minimized denominational distinctives and encouraged churchgoers to see one denomination as being as valuable as another, created an unprecedented opportunity and desire to venture out and try new churches in different traditions.

As a result, children are now less likely to follow in their parents' denominational footsteps, meaning that the loyalty of each new generation must be won rather than inherited. Among evangelicals this phenomenon has also been fostered by such para-church organizations as Youth for Christ, Gideons, Campus Crusade for Christ, Wycliffe Bible Translators, and others. Through these nondenominational contacts, Christians began feeling comfortable with other Christians from different denominations and thereby lowered their resistance to changing churches. Often young people from different denominations met through such para-church associations and married. Such marriages tended to move at least one partner to a new denomination and often moved both to the neutral turf of a third denomination or an independent church.

This era of geographical mobility has also been an era of upward mobility in social class, economic standing, and education, which often creates a desire to change to a religious alignment more in keeping with one's new status in society. There is an interesting statistical discrepancy between the numbers of Presbyterians and Southern Baptists. The Southern

Baptist convention claims several million more members than indicated by independent pollsters. Just the opposite is true with Presbyterians—millions more claim to be Presbyterian than total membership records indicate. It may well be that Presbyterianism is seen as a more prestigious denominational label by upwardly mobile Americans.

2. A decline in the number of students attending denominational colleges has also added to denominational decline. Many who once would have had their denominational ties reinforced by their collegiate experience are now attending state and secular colleges and universities or nondenominational schools. Often denominational colleges are given an impossible mandate by the officials at headquarters: "Make your students loyal to the denomination." However, many of the students on the denominational college campus are not from the denomination; they chose the school for geographical or educational opportunities rather than for its denominational stance.

Also, the rise of nondenominational Bible colleges and seminaries has flooded churches with pastors who did not grow up within the denomination they now pastor. Often these pastors are less than enthusiastic about promoting denominational loyalty because they have little themselves. While technically their churches are affiliated with a denomination, functionally they are nondenominational. Some denominations have attempted to correct this situation by refusing ordination to candidates who lack a degree from their seminaries; or, they require that graduates of other seminaries spend at least a year on the denominational seminary campus. At best, these efforts have been weak; at worst, they have been counterproductive. Rather than seeking the best person for the position, they have made denominational credentials the primary qualification for pastoral leadership.

3. On other fronts, the charismatic renewal movement resulted in major shifts in membership. In many instances individual members transferred to independent charismatic churches or Pentecostal denominations, and in some cases entire churches withdrew from their old-line denominations. Since churches are social organizations with webs of relational

connections, departing parishioners often draw others along
with them.

4. However, the greatest factor in denominational decline
is the rise of consumerism and consumer advocacy in American
culture. Consumer advocacy began with the publication of *Unsafe at Any Speed* by Ralph Nader, moving from unsafe Chevrolet Corvairs to almost every product and service in the country, resulting in a major shift in consumer consciousness.

Joe's father and grandfather always bought Ford cars; Joe
buys the car that meets his specific requirements, even if that
means buying a product not made in America. If the family
doctor's receptionist puts Mary on hold too many times, she'll
find another doctor. If Bridgestone tires are cheaper than Mich-
elin tires, Bob will switch to Bridgestone. If the public school
isn't educating their children to their satisfaction, Tom and
Linda will start looking at private schools as an alternative.

What goes for cars, doctors, tires, and schools also goes for
churches. Americans go where they think they can get the best
deal, or where they think their needs will be met, regardless
of previous affiliations.

This means that a few weeks of poor sermons, weak music,
or a dirty nursery may prompt present members to start looking
elsewhere. Guaranteed constituencies are rapidly becoming a
thing of the past.

At the same time there has been a mushrooming of churches
that are meeting expectations, particularly among independent, fundamental, charismatic, conservative, and non-
mainline churches. Those denominational churches that have
succeeded in attracting and keeping people often appear to be
out of step within their denomination. In fact, there is often
tension if not hostility between denominational headquarters
and successful denominational churches. Some of the most
prominent examples are successful conservative churches
within declining liberal denominations.

To many people the denomination is something of an ecclesiastical dinosaur that should be extinct by now. Denominations are perceived as expensive structures from an earlier
era that do not adequately serve the present generation. This

makes denominational leadership a tough job. It is yet to be seen whether declining denominations will be able to renew and revive, or whether they will die and be replaced by different structures in the next century.

The Large Church

There are an estimated 375,000 churches in the United States, and most of them are small. Half of these churches have 75 or less at worship on a typical Sunday morning. Most are surprisingly stable and indestructible and would probably continue to meet even if the pastor died, the building burned, and the treasury went bust. They are built upon and held together by permanent family relationships.

Some statisticians contend that there are actually as many as 500,000 churches in the United States. The difference in the estimates can be attributed to the varying definitions of "church," along with the existence of many home churches, storefront churches, and others so small that they are unlikely to be included in any count. The point is: Most churches are small.

However, a corresponding fact is that the majority of the church-going populace attend the larger churches. In *The Small Church Is Different*, Lyle Schaller claims that half of all worshipers are in the one-seventh largest churches in the country. Another way of saying this is that 50% of the people are in the 14% of the churches that are largest.

Large doesn't necessarily mean a congregation of thousands. In order to be in the top 5% size-wise, a church must average 250 at Sunday morning worship services. In fact, technically any church averaging more than 75 could be counted in the top half and call itself "one of the larger churches in the country"!

What is important is that there has been a significant shift in size. Management expert Peter Drucker says that the large church phenomenon is one of the major social changes in America in the twentieth century.

The move from smaller to larger is not limited to churches.

Some say it began in the 1950s with the national movement to consolidate schools and school districts. Where once each town had its own schoolhouse (even if all the grades were in one room with one teacher), many small schools consolidated into one regional school, gaining the advantages of larger enrollments and more services.

About the same time, the old "Ma and Pa" grocery stores began to disappear, replaced by supermarkets and national chains of convenience stores. Many family farms were swallowed up into agricultural conglomerates, and even physicians began practicing in medical groups or clinics.

Locally owned banks were threatened as large bank holding companies gained increasing control over the banking industry. Deregulation initially added new airlines to the transportation industry, but the tide soon turned to a very few, very large commercial carriers, swallowing up smaller lines like Frontier, Allegheny, Republic and Southern.

Many people bemoan these changes. They yearn for the old days and the old ways. They talk about "smaller is better," and may even react by seeking out smaller churches, banks, and schools. But even those who don't like it usually end up taking their business to the larger companies and institutions for one simple reason: service. In our consumer society, service has become more important than size. Most Americans want a "full service bank" that offers MasterCard or an equivalent, automatic teller machines, drive-up windows, and international travelers' cheques.

The same goes for churches. More and more Americans are opting for "full service churches" that can offer quality and variety in music, extensive youth programs, diverse educational opportunities, a counseling staff, support groups, singles' ministry, athletic activities, multiple Sunday morning services, a modern nursery, and the other services and programs only available in larger churches.

Larger churches have less need for denominations; in fact, many become "mini-denominations" in themselves. They tend to be more consumer-responsive and afford a comfortable environment for the many Americans who have grown up in high schools with thousands of students, universities with tens of thousands, companies with large payrolls and employee ano-nymity, urban apartment buildings, and suburban neighbor-hoods. As seventy-six million baby boomers move into middle age (the traditional time for returning to religion), they are likely to be attracted to larger churches (we'll see why later), thus continuing this pattern into the beginning of the next century.

Like it or not, large churches are a reality. They are drawing the majority of people, and big churches are getting bigger. Mega-churches of tens of thousands exert an increasingly pow-erful influence on everything from local politics to national religious publications.

Reshaping the Pastoral Role

In the 1700s many parishioners called the minister "Par-son," a derivation of the English word "person," because the minister was often considered THE person in the community. He was often the best educated, best read, and best traveled individual anyone knew and was held in high esteem. Through the years the pastoral role diminished. Today, however, it is taking on a new significance.

For one thing, the pastor-centered church has become com-mon. In 1950 people chose churches on the basis of denomi-nation and location; in 1990 most choose churches on the basis of the pastor. Parishioners leave a church if they don't like the pastor, even if it means driving farther and changing denom-inations.

In the area of leadership, an interesting contrast exists be-tween the church and the para-church. Following World War II, churches prospered and membership reached record highs in the United States. For the most part this prosperity was more institutional than pastoral. In other words, the churches grew as institutions, but not specifically because of who the pastor was. Not that pastors were unimportant or incompetent. On the contrary, a number of capable and committed clergy played an essential role in the church growth that occurred during the

1950s . . . Harold John OcKenga in Boston, Donald Grey Barnhouse in Philadelphia, and Bishop Fulton Sheen in New York. However, comparatively few well-known pastors built churches around their gifts and personalities.

The late 1940s and the 1950s were also a period of growth for para-church organizations, founded and led by extraordinarily gifted, charismatic, visionary leaders. Although this was certainly a fertile period for such organizations, they succeeded largely because of their leaders. So while churches were institutionally based, para-church organizations were leader based. Forty years later, this trend has been reversed.

Many para-church organizations are past their peak. The original leaders have been replaced or soon will be, and the organizations that have survived tend to continue on institutional momentum rather than being driven or led by charismatic leadership. On the flip side are the large churches often identified by the name of the pastor rather than the name of the church. Although they are prospering, these pastor-centered churches have introduced some significant risks.

For the especially gifted preacher and popular church leader, it becomes a matter of pressure and the temptation to power and pride. If he is the reason people come to the church, there is potential for him to hold unhealthy control over the congregation. If he sins, he is more likely to get away with it because the lay leadership knows that revenues and attendance could disappear if the preacher were to be disciplined. This environment is a perfect breeding ground for personality cults. Such cases have received broad publicity and have caused painful disgrace and terrible destruction. Fortunately such situations are the exception rather than the rule. It can even be argued that the negative examples have had a positive effect, making character, moral integrity, and holiness a high priority.

Perhaps the greatest effect of pastor-centered churches has been felt by those perceived as less gifted. It is increasingly difficult to hold on to people through pastoral faithfulness, church location, or denominational affiliation. So the pastor who does not meet the expectations of present and prospective parishioners faces loss of membership as well as a career crisis.

And what about the pastor who preaches a biblical and prophetic message people don't want to hear? No longer can he
expect the congregation to stick around and listen. They will
leave and go where they can hear a message they like.

The American clergy today faces unprecedented expectations. Pastors are expected to be informed, articulate, and charismatic. They are to be as attractive and well-groomed as the
anchormen on the network news, and they are expected to
relate to the peculiarities of the community. They are to attract
people, raise money, and expand programs.

I often receive letters from churches asking me to recommend pastoral candidates. Almost always two qualifications top
the list: the candidate must be an excellent preacher and an
excellent administrator. Unfortunately, those two gifts are often mutually exclusive. In addition, most churches are looking
for pastors under fifty, and a substantial number of churches
are unwilling to even consider a pastoral candidate over fifty-
five.

Ironically, just as church expectations are on the rise, the
quality of the clergy seems to be waning. Churches, in increasing numbers, are terminating their pastors. The Southern Baptist Convention, America's largest Protestant group, reports
that 116 pastors per month have their calls terminated by their
churches. That is a 31% increase since 1984. Most other denominations are also experiencing increased clergy-church
conflicts resulting in pastoral terminations.

As Martha Sawyer Allen reported in the *Minneapolis Star
Tribune*:

> America's Catholic and Protestant religious leaders
> fear that because fewer bright young people are choos-
> ing the ministry as a career, the nation's moral leader-
> ship could be seriously damaged in the 1990s and be-
> yond.
>
> "The ministry isn't as highly valued in our secular
> society anymore," said Fred Hofheinz, who is heading
> a $5 million national study of the quality of the clergy
> for the Lily Endowment. "Clearly it's a less prestigious
> profession now."

Religious leaders point to enrollment declines at seminaries nationwide as evidence that the ministry is not a desirable profession. "We really touched a nerve when the Lily Endowment began its national study," Hofheinz said. "People told us we were saying what they dared not say, but were thinking."

The Rev. Margaret Thomas, executive director of the Minnesota Council of Churches and a Presbyterian sociologist said, "A lot of us are finding that recent seminary graduates are average. In the past, graduates used to be some of the best people in American society."[1]

What is happening? And why?

One significant factor is money. Pastoral salaries are usually low, especially when compared to the salaries of other professions with comparable educational preparation. This is a negative incentive to a younger generation motivated more by money than ideals. Those who do prepare for the ministry often finish college or seminary owing thousands of dollars in school loans. These along with the normal costs of living add up to salary requirements that cannot be met by smaller churches. This unfortunate reality leaves the small church (often a rural church) with the impossible choice of either no pastor or an unqualified pastor.

A seeming contradiction to these problems is the rapid growth of multiple-pastor church staffs.

Mutiple-Pastor Staffs

In the 1950s only the largest churches had more than one pastor. Today the rule of thumb is one full-time pastor for every 150 people (based on the average Sunday morning worship attendance). This proliferation of specialized staff positions has contributed greatly to the reshaping of the professional pastoral ministry in America.

To understand this, we need to understand why we have

[1]Martha Sawyer Allen, "Church Leaders Fear Effects of Declining Seminary Enrollment," *Minneapolis Star Tribune*, (January 4, 1990), 1B, 4b. Used with permission.

so many associate pastors today.

1. One answer is that people are available. The popularity of Christianity, the growth of churches, and the baby boom (births from 1946 through 1964) filled colleges and seminaries with men and women bent on clergy careers. The Vietnam War added many men who preferred a seminary deferment to the military draft. As these new graduates flooded the job market, there were more pastors than pulpits. So the market created jobs for the growing number of applicants, mostly by expanding the pastoral staffs of existing churches rather than by starting new churches.

2. But that's only part of the answer. At the same time, new para-church organizations such as Youth for Christ, Young Life, and Campus Crusade began hiring youth and education specialists to more effectively reach the growing number of young people, which the church had not been doing. Therefore, churches felt pressured to begin or expand or improve their Christian Education and youth programs. Following the lead of the para-church organizations, they sought specialists. In the 1950s and 1960s most of the new positions on church staffs were for youth workers and Christian educators. Colleges and seminaries recognized this trend and began designing programs and granting degrees for these pastoral specialties.

Today, with a declining youth population, the demographics are different. Yet many churches have kept these positions active, expecting the new youth pastor to reproduce the successes of twenty-five years ago without the same available supply of raw materials. For this reason the para-church youth ministries have suffered on two fronts: there are far fewer youth in America to reach, and many churches have taken over the responsibility for youth ministry.

3. Another reason for the increase in multiple-pastor staffs is the general increase of professional expectation and specialization within society. Medicine is probably the most identifiable example. "General practitioner" is a designation rarely heard anymore. Most physicians limit their practices to highly specialized areas such as cardiology, pediatrics, and neurology.

Specialties then have subspecialties, such as the subdivision of
rheumatology within the specialty of internal medicine, or the
subspecialty of sports medicine under the specialty of physiatry
(physical medicine).

School teachers are no longer just "teachers." Their state
certification stipulates that they specialize in either secondary,
primary, or kindergarten. Subspecialties include special education certification for teaching children with learning disabil-
ities, physical handicaps, or behavioral problems.

This age of specialization has also come to the church. In
1960 seminaries offered few degrees and few, if any, majors.
Today, even comparatively small schools offer a wide choice
of both. When once there was only a Bachelor of Divinity, now
there is Master of Divinity, Master of Arts in Christian Education, Master of Arts in Theological Studies, Doctor of Ministry and others. Majors range from pastoral ministry to counseling, church music, youth ministry, church history,
missions, church administration and many more. Further im-
pacting this are the expectations of church-goers who have been
influenced by the rest of our culture. These expectations are
far greater than any one pastor can meet. It is not possible for
one person to have either the expertise or the time to adequately
serve a larger congregation in preaching, music, youth, singles,
education, evangelism, discipleship, and a multitude of other
ministries. The result? A church staff of specialists.

The transition from the solo generalist pastor to a multiple
staff of specialized pastors has not always been smooth. Often
the senior pastor has never worked with an associate before,
and the associate is just out of college or seminary. Neither has
experience in team ministry and neither knows many positive
models. During the 1960s and the early 1970s this resulted in
great conflicts and many terminations. While the problems
have not disappeared altogether, there are more success stories.
Many of the recent graduates have grown up in larger churches
led by multiple staffs, more senior pastors were once associate
pastors themselves, and those who tried team pastorates without comfort or success have either recommitted to solo ministries or left the pastorate.

4. A final significant factor is the great increase in lay in-

volvement. This is most apparent in the Roman Catholic Church, where 41% of the parishes in the world do not have a resident priest. The shortage of priests is critical and will increase as many older priests retire and die without replacement. It is a worldwide concern, but especially evident in the United States. Catholics suffer a shortage of ministry candidates for the same reasons as Protestants, but they also face issues unique to Catholicism. For example, the requirement of celibacy is neither attractive nor reasonable to many men, so they choose other professions. Also, the priesthood was once considered a route to education, importance, and social status for sons of lower-class immigrant families. This is no longer as attractive or necessary an option in a country where more lucrative professions embodying greater status can be attained through scholarships, grants, student loans, and other means.

Notre Dame magazine observes that the priest shortage is leading to a change in focus from the centrality of the Eucharist (only a priest can celebrate the Mass) to the centrality of Scripture (laypersons may lead Bible studies). In parishes where priests are only occasionally available, laypersons take over and teach the Bible when there can be no celebration of the Mass. If this trend continues, the power of Bible truth, the increased leadership of the laity, and the diminished presence of priests may significantly alter the face and function of the Roman Catholic Church within the next twenty-five years.

A parallel movement has taken place in Protestantism. Where once the pastor was the best educated person in the community, he or she is now only rarely the best educated even in the church. Many laypersons are now very knowledgeable and articulate in theological matters, Bible study, and church leadership. This fact not only raises the expectations set for the pastor, but shifts the power base in the politics of the church.

At the same time, we are seeing a worldwide shift from hierarchy to democracy. What has happened in the Eastern-bloc countries is just part of a global desire for people to be involved in decisions that affect them. Hierarchical churches, with the clergy at the top, are increasingly out of tune with the times. Those that persist will either face conflict, decline, and change or will attract a shrinking congregation of passive followers.

The increased influence of laity is a positive change. It moves ownership of the church out of the hands of a few professionals and into the hands of the people. It does away with elitism and introduces an experiential understanding of the real needs of the people. Cloistered clergy are no longer in charge. In the best of cases, this frees pastors to specialize in areas of expertise and need. The principles of Ephesians 4:11–12 come into play as gifted leaders equip the entire church to undertake the work of the ministry.

Around the world, across the country, and within the church we are experiencing change. Some think it has barely begun and that the next changes will be more sweeping than the last. Others anticipate a conclusion to this period of transition and the dawning of an era of greater predictability and stability.

In his best-selling book *Future Shock*, Alvin Toffler said that "change is avalanching upon our heads and most people are grotesquely unprepared to cope with it."[2]

Coping begins with comprehending. Only as we understand the way our world is now and anticipate the way it will be in the future can we cope with change. But we must do more than just cope. We must contribute.

---

[2]Alvin Toffler, *Future Shock* (New York: Bantam Books, 1970), 12.

Chapter 4

You Can't Pick Your Birthday

WHEN JOHN F. KENNEDY sought the 1960 Democratic nomination for President of the United States, his Catholicism was a major consideration for many voters. However, there was another issue at stake that was even bigger than the matter of his faith and ideology, and that was his age. John Kennedy was only 43 years old. He and his generation were in competition with the older generation that controlled the Democratic party—a generation that still remembered the defeat of Catholic candidate Alfred E. Smith in 1928.

While Republican nominee Richard M. Nixon ran on the record of President Dwight D. Eisenhower, Kennedy ran on the promise to lead America to a "New Frontier." Kennedy won and in his inaugural address on January 20, 1961, he made a special point of the fact that he was the first president born in the twentieth century.

The generational issue also entered national politics in the 1988 election when George Bush chose Dan Quayle as his running mate. Quayle was born in 1947, making him the first baby boomer to run for a presidential office. Bush clearly recognized the importance of generations as he sought to win the votes of Americans born after World War II.

Generations

The year we are born has an enormous effect on the way we view the world and the way we live. There is a big difference between living through the Great Depression and just reading about it, between fighting in Vietnam and seeing it on television years later. Since persons born in the same years and even within the same decades or eras share many common experiences, they tend to become a generational group clearly differentiated from persons of another generation. This is not to say that everyone sharing a specific birthday has the same attitudes and beliefs. Obviously they do not. However, there are enough similarities to make them significant.

The study of society by generations has become big business. Americans for Generational Equity (AGE) is a nonprofit, nonpartisan educational institution that publishes *The Generational Journal*. It makes for fascinating reading, covering such topics as "The Birth Dearth: A Graying Economy," "America Faces Challenge: Four-Generation Society," "Aging and the Private Sector," and "The Intergenerational Consequences of Tax Design."[1]

On the commercial side is the *Marketing Tools Alert* by *American Demographics* magazine, a monthly catalog of books and other resources to aid one in keeping up on generational sociology and its applications in the marketplace. Some of the categories are Youth Market (born 1977 and after), Baby Bust (born 1965–1976), Baby Boom (born 1946–1964), and the 50-Plus Market. Sample offerings include:

Children as Consumers by James U. McNeil

This fascinating book examines how children learn to be consumers, their income and expenditures, why they prefer certain stores, advertising they respond to, what

[1]*The Generational Journal*, (Vol. I, No. 2, July 15, 1988).

products appeal to children, packaging and premiums for this market, and much more. A must for anyone whose fortunes are tied to the youth market. Book #646.

Beyond the Baby Boom: How Will the Baby Bust Be Different? by Matthew Greenwald

Find out who is in the post-baby-boom generation, what they want, and how to satisfy them from this in-depth discussion of generational marketing. #546 (1 cassette).

What the Baby Boom Believes by Jay Ogilvy

Get the psychographic story behind what members of the baby boom want and why from one of the most knowledgeable people in the field, who explains how their desires affect your business goals, now and in the future. #543 (1 cassette).[2]

The fact that such books even exist is repulsive to some people. More repulsive is the notion that such methods could be applied to the mission and ministry of the church. Yet generational characteristics and differences are a reality. Even the Bible recognizes the basics of generational sociology when it notes that the generation "which knew not Moses" had to be dealt with differently from the generation that had known and experienced Moses face to face.

Let's consider just a few examples of generational characteristics and their implications.

Men tend to marry women two or three years younger than themselves. This doesn't have much impact as long as there are approximately equal numbers of men and women. However, beginning in 1946 that was no longer the case, which greatly affected marriage patterns twenty years later. With the marked increase in births beginning in 1946, there were suddenly more females in ratio to the males born before 1946. Thus, beginning around 1966 there were more marriage-age women than there were men. This surplus continued for nearly

---

[2]*Marketing Tools Alert*, May 1989, P.O. Box 68, Ithaca, NY 14851.

two decades, and men had a "buyer's market." Then came the decline in births after 1964, which meant that there were far fewer females two or three years younger than the marriage-age males. Marriage switched to a "seller's market" for women. *Changing Times* magazine explains:

> When the largest pool of baby-boom women passed age 30, which happened in 1987, men seeking marriage faced a declining number of women two to three years younger. From 108 unmarried women ages 18 to 27 per 100 men in their twenties in 1970, the ratio is headed toward 93 unmarried women per 100 men in 1990.[3]

In the same article, Jib Fowles, professor of human science and humanities at the University of Houston in Clear Lake, says that the competitive pressure among men to secure women will fuel a renewed fervor among men for commitment to relationships and families.

This generational dynamic has also affected the church. For an entire generation the church operated with a surplus of single women. This led to strategies in singles' ministries targeted on getting the men in order to get the women. Mission organizations had many single women missionaries and very few single men missionaries.

More subjective but also more significant than the male-female birth ratio is the phenomenon of common experiences. Those born in the late 1920s and in the 1930s were indelibly marked by the Great Depression. It was an era of limited resources and social upheaval. There was no television. That generation lived through the threat of Hitler's advance across Europe, the bombing of Pearl Harbor, the American involvement in World War II, and the longest presidency in the history of the country. Those experiences bonded the generation together and will be with them for the rest of their lives.

Compare this to a later generation bonded together by television, prosperity, peace, multiple assassinations of national leaders, nuclear threat, the Vietnam War, Watergate, and rock-

---

[3]Daniel M. Kehrer, "5 Population Trends Every Investor Should Know," *Changing Times*, September 1988, 58.

and-roll music. Not only do they have different things to talk about, but they also have a different perspective on reality and their own generational values.

Summarizing parts of two Harvard Business School surveys, *The Boomer Report* for April 1989 says:

> Boomers were born prosperous (trust the economy) but were disillusioned by Vietnam and Watergate (don't trust government or institutions). Their parents experienced the Great Depression (don't trust the economy) but fought the good fight in WWII (trust the government). It makes for basically different values.

Shared (or unshared) experiences bond generations together. This is often such a powerful phenomenon that many individuals are completely unable to see the perspective of another generation; therefore there can be no dialogue. This can be very damaging for families, communities, businesses, and churches, which all need to operate intergenerationally. Recognizing this enables us to see why certain patterns develop in the church.

Analyst Lyle Schaller claims that persons born before 1930 are most likely to visit a new church for the first time on a Sunday morning; they are also primarily attracted to churches averaging less than 300 at worship. By contrast, those born after 1950 are much more likely to enter a new church through something other than the Sunday morning worship service— perhaps a church-sponsored Bible study class, a softball team, a Christmas Eve service, a divorce recovery workshop, an organ concert, a film series, a young adult group, or involvement in some expression of community outreach. Also, the younger generation is much more likely to be attracted to the church that averages an attendance of 1000.

Life Cycles

While each generation has its own characteristics, each generation also goes through the normal life cycle of birth, childhood, adolescence, adulthood, retirement, and death. All of these have an effect on social change.

Professor Franco Modigliani of M.I.T., winner of the 1985 Nobel prize in economics, brought his Life Cycle Theory to economics. Young adults tend to have very low savings rates because they are forming their households, have lower income, and need to acquire many basic possessions such as cars and houses. Often they are net borrowers, consuming more than they earn. Add twenty years to their ages and the same people become net savers as they now own their houses, are concerned about paying for children's education, and are trying to accumulate money for retirement.

In 1989 only 6% of U.S. savings were owned by persons aged 25–34 compared to 66% of the savings owned by persons over 55. Put this together with the population distribution and you begin to understand why America's national savings rate has dipped below 2%. We have had a period influenced by a large number of younger adults and comparatively few aged 40–60. Lots of spenders and few savers. However, as these baby boomers age, moving out of the spending cycle and into the saving cycle, many economists are predicting the debt will go down and the national savings rate may increase to 10%.

Crime rates are also affected by the life cycle. Most crimes are committed by males in late adolescence and early adulthood. Beginning in the late 1960s, this age group became the largest age group in the population. As a result, the crime rate soared. "Law and Order" led political agendas in the late 1960s and early 1970s. Now that those in the high crime years comprise a smaller segment of our population, crime rates are subsiding and political attention shifts to other issues.

Life cycles also affect church attendance and other religious activities and beliefs. Those who grow up in the church typically drop out for two to eight years during their late teens and twenties. As they get older, and especially when they have children, an estimated 80% return. *Christianity Today* says that "while Americans' worship patterns through the decades reveal a remarkable constancy, the statistics on church attendance, when viewed up close, reveal dramatic and distinctive patterns along generational lines." Then this explanation is added:

Throughout their lives, Americans born during the Depression have been more faithful than later generations in their church/synagogue attendance.

"War babies" dropped out of church as they entered their twenties during the turbulent sixties, and stayed away. The twin disillusionments stemming from Vietnam and Watergate made them more suspicious of institutions—the church included. Only recently, as they approach and pass mid-life, are they trickling back to church.

Baby boomers also dropped out of church in their twenties, but now, in their thirties and early forties, they are returning to the ranks of the faithful. The real boom in church attendance is coming from this generation.

David A. Roozen, William McKinney, and Wayne Thompson, a research team at Hartford Seminary, were among the first researchers to detect the postwar generation's return to church and synagogue. They found that the number of older baby boomers (those born between 1946 and 1958) who go to church regularly has risen from 33.5 percent in the early seventies to 42.8 percent in the early eighties—an increase of more than 9 percent. In short, these "prodigal sons and daughters," as Roozen calls them, have recovered two thirds of the drop-off of the sixties and seventies. High-income baby boomers (those making more than $30,000 a year) have returned in the greatest numbers.[4]

These church participation patterns match Robert L. Bast's descriptions in *Attracting New Members*. Using the life-cycle approach, he lists five age groups and describes how they typically function in relation to the church. (In considering these we are looking not only at the characteristics typical of the age group, but the characteristics typical of the particular generation currently filling that age group.)

Age 18–25 = Inactivity: For the most part this age group

[4]Wesley G. Pippert, "The Revival of Religion in America," *Editorial Research Reports* (Washington D.C.: Congressional Quarterly Inc., 1988), 366–375.

does not really relate to the church. They have dropped out. Research by the Alban Institute demonstrated that during the drop-out period most of these people do not stop believing and are not hostile to the church, and they do tend to make their way back into the church, usually at about age 25 or 26.

Age 26–40 = Opportunity: These are the years of return, particularly as people have children. They also comprise the bulk of the volunteer workers, "particularly in the areas of outreach and nurture." They have children in the nursery and Sunday school, so they are more likely to help out. They meet others their age through the school and sports activities of their children, which makes them effective in evangelism through relationship networks.

Age 41–55 = Leadership: This segment knows the church well, has proved itself through earlier stages, holds positions of leadership outside the church, and provides much of the financial support for the church. During the 1980s they were leaders within many churches and para-church organizations. However, this age group was born during a low birthrate period so there are fewer of them. Often their lower numbers and the fact that they have been overshadowed all of their lives by the generations before and after has made them less than the best leaders. In some cases institutional leadership has gone to the younger or older generations by default, making for a missing generation in the leadership sequence.

Age 56–65 = Loyalists: This segment of the population has made church loyalty a habit. They have been faithful for a long time and will continue to be faithful. However, they often feel they have done their duty and are ready to turn over both leadership and responsibility to those who are younger. Their children are grown, their health is good, their discretionary income is high. They like to travel and enjoy their freedom. When in town, they will attend church. They will give money. They will be supportive.

Age 65 and above = Servant and Served: Some people who are retirement age choose to serve others; some choose to be served by others. Eventually, however, even those who choose to serve age into the category of having to be served, particularly in the eighties and above, when deteriorating health, loss of spouse, and other issues severely limit the ability to serve and increase the necessity of being served.

Bast gives an example of the challenges that may come when generational and life-cycle issues mix and conflict:

People born between 1930–1945 were born during times of hardship. Depression and a world war resulted in scarcity and shortages, and massive problems produced a climate of hardship. As a result, people born during this period are likely to face life with caution. They tend to be conservers, and to believe in delayed gratification. In contrast, people born during the years 1945–1960 were born in "boom times." They grew up in a society experiencing prosperity and growth, and the climate was one of optimism. As a result, people born during this period are likely to be risk-takers, who spend money easily, and who practice instant gratification.[5]

I experienced this firsthand during my first crisis in my first pastorate. I had challenged the people of that Colorado church to make a faith promise of increased giving for world missions. To my delight they committed an additional $5,700 per year (a 50% increase over the existing missions budget). I practically floated to the missions committee meeting where we were to draft a revised budget. To my amazement there wasn't even a second to the motion for revision. The committee's attitude was summed up by one member who said, "Pastor, when the money actually comes in we'll decide where to spend it."

I didn't know whether I was hurt or angry or both. It was obvious to me that I trusted God and they did not. God, missions, and I had suffered a terrible defeat.

Years later I saw that episode in a very different light. What I thought was a spiritual issue, I now see as a generational issue. It was not that I trusted God and they did not. The difference

---

[5]Robert L. Bast, *Attracting New Members* (co-published by New York: Reformed Church in America, and Honrovia, Calif.: Church Growth, Inc., 1988), 32.

was that they had lived through the Great Depression and I had not.

Such a reaction is typical of the enormous problem most of us face in dealing with generational and life-cycle issues: We cannot see outside our own generational ghetto. Even when we can, it may be almost impossible to really comprehend the mix of experiences, values, and priorities of someone from another generation.

Have you seen women wearing the sweatshirt that says "I'd Rather Be 40 Than Pregnant"? It's tough for a 26-year-old woman wanting a baby to understand why another woman would wear such a statement. It is equally difficult for the woman in the sweatshirt—who has changed more diapers than she ever thought she would see, is struggling with children in adolescence, and finally thinks she understands what life is all about—to count anyone wanting to become pregnant as sane. It's all a matter of generations and life cycles. It's all a matter of perspective.

All of this becomes a very practical concern to churches and Christian organizations. Consider a church that is located near a Florida or Arizona retirement community. The good news is that most of the parishioners are from the same generation and share the same values, reducing the likelihood of conflict. They tend to look at life in similar ways and accept programs geared to their generation. The bad news is that there often is a shortage of leaders and servants, for many have passed those stages in their life-cycle progression.

Many older para-church organizations with strong ministries in evangelism and education face this same situation. Their constituency has aged with the organization, and this strong and loyal donor base insists on perpetuating values and styles that do not attract a younger generation. The net effect may eventually destroy the ministry.

At the other extreme are younger churches and organizations that have plenty of workers but few experienced leaders and very limited funding. This scenario is evident in the booming young church that cannot afford adequate facilities and staff to properly minister to all the people.

The best of all worlds is an intergenerational balance, with enough persons in each life-cycle segment and from each generation to fulfill the mission of the organization. Since the ideal rarely exists, each organization must analyze its generational distribution, assessing strengths and weaknesses, and establish a strategy that will best enable it to fulfill its mission with the resources available. In some extreme situations, fulfillment of mission may be impossible, and the courageous strategy will be to close or to merge.

Pre-World War II

When taking a closer look at specific generations, it quickly becomes evident that persons born before World War II have dominated the country and its institutions for most of the twentieth century. They have lived longer, experienced more, and are the most powerful in terms of position and money.

Every president of the United States, most CEO's of major corporations, heads of denominations, presidents of leading colleges, and other significant leaders were born before World War II. Their generation experienced the disillusionment brought on by the Great Depression, which followed an earlier period of unrealistic optimism. The failure of banks and businesses taught economic caution, self-reliance, hard work, and rather liberal politics. Next came World War II, which the United States was slow to enter because of the popular isolationist belief that it was a European war and we were better off staying out of it. When Europe systematically fell to the Axis powers and the Japanese attacked Pearl Harbor, politics quickly changed. The once reluctant nation declared war and fought with fervor, deploying military forces overseas and mobilizing a wartime economy at home. America succeeded not only in winning the war but in reviving the economy, entering the nuclear age, and dominating much of the world with its political influence.

These experiences and actions produced the post-war economic prosperity and peace of the 1950s. While that decade also marked the beginning of the Cold War, it was mostly a happy time in America. This convinced the pre-World War II generation that its values were valid. Sacrifice, hard work, patriotism, and liberal politics had paid off. All the next generation needed to do for further success was build on the foundation they had provided and perpetuate the values they offered.

The values of this significant and influential generation are clearly evident in a clever statement by an unknown author entitled "For All Those Born Before 1945."

WE ARE SURVIVORS!!!! Consider the changes we have witnessed:

We were born before television, before penicillin, before polio shots, frozen foods, Xerox, plastic, contact lenses, Frisbees and the Pill.

We were before radar, credit cards, split atoms, laser beams and ballpoint pens, before pantyhose, dishwashers, clothes dryers, electric blankets, air conditioners, drip-dry clothes—and before anyone walked on the moon.

We got married first and then lived together. How quaint can you be?

In our time, closets were for clothes, not for "coming out of." Bunnies were small rabbits and rabbits were not Volkswagens. Designer Jeans were scheming girls named Jean or Jeanne, and having a meaningful relationship meant getting along well with our cousins.

We thought fast food was what you ate during Lent, and Outer Space was the back of the Riviera Theater.

We were before house-husbands, gay rights, computer dating, dual careers and commuter marriages. We were before day-care centers, group therapy and nursing homes. We never heard of FM radio, tape decks, electric typewriters, artificial hearts, word processors, yogurt, and guys wearing earrings. For us, time-sharing meant togetherness—not computers or condominiums; a "chip" meant a piece of wood; hardware meant hardware, and software wasn't even a word!

In 1940, "made in Japan" meant junk and the term "making out" referred to how you did on your exam. Pizzas, McDonald's and instant coffee were unheard of. We hit the scene when there were 5 and 10 cent stores, where you bought things for five and ten cents. Sanders and Wilson sold ice cream cones for a nickel or a dime. For one nickel you could ride a street car, make a phone call, buy a Pepsi or enough stamps to mail one letter and two post cards. You could buy a new Chevy Coupe for $600, but who could afford one? A pity, too, for gas was 11 cents a gallon.

In our day, cigarette smoking was fashionable. Grass was mowed. Coke was a cold drink and pot was something you cooked in. Rock music was a grandma's lullaby and aids were helpers in the principal's office.

We were certainly not before the difference between the sexes was discovered, but we were surely before the sex change. We made do with what we had. And we were the last generation that was so dumb as to think you needed a husband to have a baby!

No wonder we are so confused and there is such a generation gap today!

BUT WE SURVIVED!!!! What better reason to celebrate?

Not every word is accurate, nor is every value shared by those born before World War II. But the author communicates a generational solidarity that is real. Indeed, the pre-war generation did more than survive, it succeeded.

Then came the baby boom.

Chapter 5

Baby Boomers: A Generation Apart

IN 1985 COCA-COLA introduced "New Coke," a move that left many scratching their heads and wondering, "What's wrong with the old Coke?" What was wrong was that in the soft-drink world Coca-Cola's major competitor Pepsi appeared to be gobbling up the market share with their sweeter, less fizzy product. Evidence indicated that younger consumers preferred their cola sweeter and less fizzy. Since teenagers were the age group that consumed the most soft drinks, it was logical to cater to their tastes. So the summer of 1985 saw many families conducting their own blindfolded cola tests to see which they liked the best.

The results were a fizzle.

Both Pepsi and Coke had neglected to consider the massive market of baby boomers, the youngest of whom turned 21 in 1985. They liked the "real thing," the taste of the Coke they'd grown up with. As many as 1500 phone calls a day protested the change to New Coke. Petitions were circulated. Coke loyalists bought up remaining supplies and hoarded them.

After three months of this consumer reaction, the Coca-

Cola company brought back the tried and true under the label Coke Classic. And today it is tough to find a can of New Coke.

"American businesses learned a lesson from the Coca-Cola fiasco," says baby boomer Cheryl Russell. "Though youth was once the most important consumer market in the United States, it no longer holds the power. Because of the middle-aging of the baby boom, older Americans now control the marketplace. But the baby boom also realized that it was no longer the new generation."[1]

Baby boomers hold a disproportionate influence over our entire society—from our cola to our churches. In fact, their influence is even greater than their numbers. They consume 51% of all the goods and services in America; and 81% of America's journalists are baby boomers, bringing their perspectives and prejudices into almost everything others read and see in the news. Older and younger generations increasingly must go along with the ways of the baby boomer, who is now "the average American."

> The "average" American is Jane (not John) Doe. And she's a boomer. She is a 32-year-old woman who makes less than $20,000/year in a technical, sales or administrative job. Standing 5'4", she weighs 143 pounds and is dieting. She owns an 8-year-old blue sedan that gets 18 miles/gallon and costs $3,000/year to own and operate.[2]

"Baby boomers" have certainly become a household word in the United States in recent years. But just who are they?

The Baby Boom

Although they haven't been babies for a long time, the generation born from 1946 through 1964 will be known as "the Baby Boom" generation until the last boomer dies sometime in the last half of the twenty-first century. During those nine-

---

[1]Cheryl Russell, *100 Predictions for the Baby Boom*, (New York: Plenum Press, 1987), 49.
[2]Paul C. Light, *Baby Boomers*, (New York: W. W. Norton Company, 1988).

Baby Boomers: A Demographic Profile

This chart highlights Boomer adults according to major demographic qualifications. Indicated are comparisions of Boomers among themselves, as well as against various total U.S. demographic groups. The third column demonstrates the degree to which Boomers tend to represent the demography in comparison to total adults 18 and over.

	% of Baby Boomers	% of Total Adults	% More Likely Than Total Adults
Sex			
Male	49.3%	47.7%	3%
Female	50.7	52.3	−3
Education			
College Graduate +	24.7	18.4	34
Attended College +	45.9	36.7	25
High School Graduate +	85.3	76.4	12
Occupation			
Professional/Managerial	23.2	16.6	40
Household Income			
$40,000 +	34.4	30.3	13
$30,000–39,999	54.3	47.0	15
$25,000–29,999	64.5	55.9	15
$20,000–24,999	10.3	10.2	1
$15,000–19,999	7.3	8.5	−14
Marital Status			
Married	66.4	60.5	10
Single	19.2	21.5	−11
Widowed, Divorced/Separated	14.4	18.0	−20
Presence of Children			
No Children	37.2	59.7	−38
Any Children	62.8	40.3	56
1–2 Children	46.4	31.4	48
3–4 Children	14.8	8.0	85
4 + Children	5.5	3.0	83

Source: The Expert's Guide to The Baby Boomers (Update), PEOPLE Magazine/SMRB 1989

teen years, 75,873,000 Americans were born. Amazingly, their numbers have increased since—because of immigration. By 1988 there were 77,268,000 baby boomers. Based on an estimated 1989 U.S. population of 248,241,000, baby boomers represent 31.1% of the total. In other words, nearly one third of all Americans now living were born between 1946 and 1964.

When 3.4 million babies were born in 1946, it was a 20% increase over 1945. Demographers thought it was a one-year phenomenon due to soldiers returning from the war, but the boom could not be so easily explained, nor did it stop there. The peak year was 1957 with 4.3 million births. And from 1954 through 1964 each year had at least 4 million births.

Many explanations have been offered, but no one has convinced population experts that any single answer is correct. It seems that many factors merged in America for nearly twenty years: more marriages, younger marriages, women having babies younger, women having more babies, economic prosperity, peace, and positive outlook for the future.

The Population Reference Bureau summarizes the phenomenon this way: "Simply put, the baby boom was a 'disturbance' which emanated from a decade-and-a-half-long fertility splurge on the part of American couples. The post-World War II phenomenon upset what had been a century-long decline in the U.S. fertility rate."[3] The decline in fertility after the baby boom represents a return to normal more than an exception to the norm.

The baby boomer generation created a "pig in a python" effect on American society and particularly on the surrounding, smaller generations. (By way of comparison, only 24.4 million live births were recorded in the U.S. in the 1930s.) When the boomers first arrived there was a shortage of schools, so many were built; when the last boomers finished public school, there was a surplus of schools. When the first boomers entered college, they created fierce competition for too few spots, so colleges and universities expanded (many were even founded during this period). After the last boomers graduated, colleges and

---

[3]Light, op. cit.

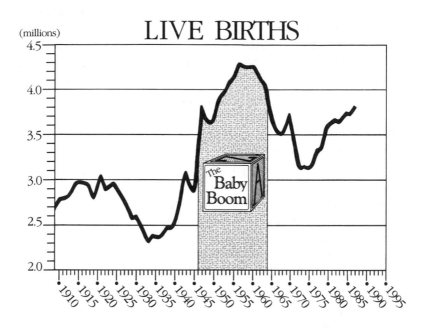

LIVE BIRTHS

(millions)

universities suffered from a shortage of students, and many had to close. When baby boomers moved into the job market, unemployment soared. After they all procured jobs, unemployment dropped. We may expect the same shocking effect when baby boomers retire, move into nursing homes, and die.

Madison Avenue advertisers took notice, and the youth culture reigned as businesses competed for the big baby boomer market. Most ads featured the young. However, now that baby boomers are aging, the market is adjusting to products and ads targeted to the middle-aged.

As baby boomers age, the whole face of the nation is changing. After the year 2000 there will be more old people than young people in the United States—for the first time in history. Futurists disagree on the future impact of the baby boomers. Some say they will live longer, healthier, and happier than any previous generation. Others contend that they will not age gracefully: they will overwhelm the social and medical capabilities of our society, polarize generations, bankrupt Social Security, succumb to Alzheimer's Disease in large numbers, and create general chaos.

One thing is certain, though: baby boomers will continue to dominate American society for decades to come. Their sheer numbers guarantee it.

However, we must be careful not to assume that all baby boomers are alike. A span of nineteen years in the fast-changing last half of the twentieth century has forced sub-segmentation of this generation. Those born in 1946 either fought in Vietnam or stayed home and protested against the war. Those born in 1964 don't even remember the Vietnam War. A woman born in 1946 could have a daughter born in 1964 and they would both be baby boomers, although they are a literal generation apart.

Political science professor Paul C. Light gives some helpful insights in this regard:

> They grew up as the first standardized generation, drawn together by the history around them, the intimacy of television, and the crowding that came from the sheer onslaught of other baby boomers. They shared the great economic expectations of the 1950s and the fears that came with Sputnik and the dawn of the nuclear era. They shared the hopes of John F. Kennedy's New Frontier and Lyndon Johnson's Great Society, and the disillusionment that came with assassinations, Vietnam, Watergate, and the resignations. To the extent these memories remain fresh, the baby boom will be a generation united.[4]

Professor Light adds that generational solidarity is based on much more than shared birth dates. "They reflect a shared sense of time, a shared feeling for an era. German sociologist Karl Mannheim called such a shared feeling a zeitgeist—a spirit of the times." Of course, this could be said of any generation.

---

[4]Light, op. cit.

However, Light argues that "the baby boomers have a perception of themselves as being very different from other generations—a perception that has existed from childhood."

What may be genuinely unique about them is that baby boomers were the first "standardized" generation in America. Light writes:

> They grew up in the standardized kitchens and houses that came with the building codes of the 1940s, studied the standardized curricula that came with the drive for universal access to education of the 1950s, and lived with the standardized fear that came with atomic bomb drills and the Vietnam War in the 1960s. They were battered by the nonstop advertising that catered a deep need for privacy and individual distinction. There is no doubt that the baby boomers shared a unique childhood and adolescence which marks them even today.[5]

Baby boomers consciously think of themselves as different from the previous generation. As a result, they operate differently and expect to be treated differently. Those who are baby boomers may instinctively understand this; others need to study this generation as a distinct subculture. Even some of the older baby boomers themselves, educated and trained to think in the patterns of an earlier generation, must be reeducated if they are to adequately understand and relate to their own generational peers.

Whatever our orientation, it is both valuable and vital that we identify and understand the characteristics of this generation that exerts such great influence on our society and, consequently, on our churches.

Low Loyalty

The Depression generation is known for its brand-loyalty. Grandpa bought his first Ford in 1938, and he has been buying

---

[5]Light, op. cit.

Fords ever since. He may even keep his savings in the same First National Bank he has patronized since he got his first job. It didn't fail in 1929, and he has expressed his gratitude with unswerving loyalty ever since.

What goes for cars and banks goes for churches as well. Grandpa and Grandma have stuck with the Lutheran Church on Elm Street through good times and bad. They were baptized and married there, as were their parents before them. Changing churches or denominations is unthinkable, even if attendance is down and the new minister is too liberal. Loyalty is a virtue.

Neither Grandpa nor Grandma can comprehend the lack of institutional loyalty they see in their thirty-four-year-old son and daughter-in-law. If they can get one-quarter percent higher interest at some unknown bank in Texas, they will readily transfer their savings half-way across the country. Saving a few dollars or getting a better warranty motivates their son to trade in a perfectly good Ford on a Korean-made Hyundai. And their daughter-in-law started the family attending a big Assembly of God church just because of a high-powered children's program.

The older generation can't understand their adult children's lack of institutional loyalty. And the younger generation can't comprehend their parents' devotion that will settle for lesser quality out of blind loyalty.

All of this goes a long way toward explaining the numerical decline of churches that have expected loyalty but neglected needs; and it explains the significant growth of nondenominational churches that have catered to the perceived needs of baby boomers. More and more churches are moving away from denominational labels to neutral names such as Christ Church or Montclair Community Church. Even churches with denominational affiliations are minimizing their labels in order to attract baby boomers.

Akin to low loyalty is the trend toward nonaffiliation. In the 1950s church membership was in vogue even for those who seldom attended church. In the 1990s many regular attenders never become church members. Several different factors account for this phenomenon:

1. The attitude that needs outweigh loyalty, which means a willingness to switch to another church if needs will be met there;

2. Increased perception of any specific church as a "way station" on one's ongoing spiritual journey rather than a final destination;

3. Openness to upward job mobility, which may require changing location;

4. Loyalty to a specific minister rather than to a local church or denomination.

Pastor loyalty rather than church or denominational loyalty is frequent. Many baby boomers don't trust institutions but do trust individuals. If the pastor is credible and trustworthy, the label on the church sign doesn't matter as much.

High Expectations

It may seem contradictory that baby boomers who aren't loyal to institutions have high expectations of those same institutions. Contradiction or not, it is a characteristic of this generation. Those born after World War II have grown up with a sense of entitlement. They have been taught that government, education, medicine, marriage, and religion should all function with excellence.

The past forty years have produced stunning accomplishments. Medical research has erased smallpox, nearly eliminated polio, and made organ transplants routine. We have come to believe that any malady can be cured. That's why baby boomers expect cures for cancer and AIDS and become frustrated when those do not seem immediately forthcoming.

The same period brought equally high expectations of education. Better schools, teachers, and curricula have been promoted as the instruments for overcoming poverty and effecting overall social change.

Baby boomers have a lot and expect a lot. Dr. Martin E. P. Seligman, professor of psychology at the University of Pennsylvania, writes about these expectations in his article "Boomer Blues":

Our soaring expectations went beyond consumer goods into nonmaterial matters. We came to expect our jobs to be more than a way to make a living. Work now needs to be ecologically innocent, comfortable to our dignity, a call to growth and excitement, a meaningful contribution to society—and deliver a large paycheck. Married partners once settled for duty, but mates today expect to be ecstatic lovers, intellectual colleagues and partners in tennis and water sports. We even expect our partners to be loving parents, a historical peculiarity to anyone versed in the Victorian child-rearing model.[6]

Some say that greater education produces greater expectations. If that is so, baby boomers qualify for high expectations indeed. They are the best-educated generation in history. One reason for this is the fact that the Vietnam War kept more people (especially males with student deferments) in college longer.

Ironically, these high expectations have often led to failure rather than success, as evidenced by increased divorces (more than half of all baby boomer marriages will end in divorce), military desertion, and church dropout. Reality cannot possibly measure up to such great expectations. So when a marriage doesn't measure up to the baby boomer's high ideals, she bails out. When the government doesn't conduct a war in accordance with the baby boomer's standards, he goes AWOL. When a church fails to provide spiritual revitalization, the boomer family looks elsewhere. As a result, depression has increased tenfold in the last two decades as people struggle to cope with the disappointments of unmet expectations.

Not the least of these disappointments is the boomers' failure to meet their own expectations. They have found themselves in a highly competitive world with 77,000,000 others vying for the same jobs, houses, and money. Many peaked early in their careers and have nowhere else to go. Unlike past generations, which pegged their hopes to the greater successes of their children, baby boomers are now being told that their

---

[6]Martin E. P. Seligman, "Boomer Blues," *Psychology Today*, October, 1988.

children will probably not do as well as the parents.

However, this situation offers two positives for the church: (1) those institutions that meet the baby boomers' high expectations will flourish; and (2) baby boomers tend to respond well to institutions that have high expectations of them.

Churches that have targeted the baby boomers provide quality programs and facilities; they are committed to excellence but do not require blind loyalty. They strive to communicate on a level comparable to that which the baby boomer experiences in the best of the secular world. The church nursery rivals the day-care center down the street for attractiveness and cleanliness. Sermons are compelling and credible for the college-educated parishioner who is both well-read and well-traveled. High standards are maintained, whether in the matter of biblical truth and or in the quality of Christian fellowship.

In a church like this, baby boomers find a place where the failures of other institutions are momentarily forgotten and where they can experience a heightened sensitivity to and understanding of God. No doubt this demands a great deal of the church, but is this not consistent with the high standards of God?

Boomers have grown up in an extraordinarily competitive environment—too many people competing for too few openings. Teachers have expected the best. Coaches have told them to hustle or be cut from the team. Employers regularly remind them that there are others willing to take their place.

The baby boomer should feel "right at home" in the church that holds high expectations of its people, including church membership and attendance, devotional disciplines, service inside and outside the church, financial support, social responsibility, and Christian lifestyle. Baby boomers want to be challenged, and many of them will be attracted to such a church even if they won't join, give, or serve. They like the idea of high expectations even if they don't personally comply.

High expectations alone are not enough; in fact, in themselves they will probably eventually drive people away. With these high expectations must come the provision of enablement to meet them. Enablement includes teaching, training, counseling, support, discipline, role models, classes, books, and other tools. This care creates an environment in which the boomer can feel positive about the church and about self, which opens the way to even higher expectations.

Weaker Relationships

This generation has not been a good one for building strong relationships. In the midst of the huge population curve, many people live in isolation and anonymity.

Mobility has divided up the extended family. Few people still live on the farm or in the neighborhood where they grew up. Competition in the classroom and the marketplace has fostered a generation of individualists who know they must make it on their own. And what should be the closest relationship of life—that of husband and wife—has become the greatest disappointment. High divorce rates evidence this fact and bring in compounding factors, which only increase the loneliness and isolation.

Divorce consumes time, money, and energy. First there is the matter of ending the marriage and determining custody of any children. Then one must either raise the children as a single parent, or work out a shared custody lifestyle. Financial resources must be divided between two households, requiring more hours devoted to earning money and maintaining two careers.

Because many baby boomers see the world as a hostile and difficult place, they have increased their cocooning instincts (staying home). All of these and other factors either strain existing relationships or prevent the nurturing of new ones.

Numerous studies have concluded that women have better relational skills and thus have better success in developing and maintaining friendships with each other. The American male, however, is often "friendless." Circumstances of the generation combine with natural male competitiveness to leave many isolated.

Noticing this generational characteristic and societal trend, the commercial market has attempted to use it to advantage.

Dating services have been commercially successful, but clubs and service organizations have not done well. Churches have addressed this need for building relationships by promoting family values and establishing networks of fellowship and support groups. The small group movement has flourished and looks even more promising for the future. This is a need that the church is uniquely qualified to meet.

Many of the most successful church models are based on addressing multiple needs through special groups. For example, Adult Children of Alcoholics support groups draw adults who grew up in alcoholic homes. This type of group meets a primary need, but is also an effective structure for developing friendships. Similar approaches are used with athletic teams, music groups, parenting classes, employment services, cancer support groups, and Bible study classes. Many traditional adult Sunday school programs continue to emphasize Bible study, but really function more as opportunities for fellowship.

Tolerance for Diversity

We live in a multiple choice world. With access to more magazines, more TV channels, and more restaurants—to name just a few—the multiplicity of available choices is truly staggering. This kind of diversity carries over into every area of life, and for the first time, with the baby boomers, we have a generation with tolerance for such diversity. Cheryl Russell says:

> Though the baby boom is no monolith, it is united in its tolerance of diversity. The educational level of the baby boom makes it more accepting and even encouraging of individual differences and alternative lifestyles. The result is an increasingly diverse American culture in which single women have children through artificial insemination, avowed homosexuals run for public office, divorced parents have joint custody of their children, and people marry two or even three times without raising an eyebrow.[7]

---
[7]Russell, op. cit.

Acceptance of diversity is something baby boomers practice intuitively rather than consciously. If they are conscious of it at all, it is more a sense that they are supposed to expect a broad array of choices and even contradiction of lifestyles. People have a "right" to such diversity.

Thus, baby boomers feel at home in huge, multi-level shopping malls where there are stores they will never visit. They expect employers to offer a "cafeteria plan" of fringe benefits rather than a pre-structured package. Even in school it is normal to have course choices offered from kindergarten through high school.

Boomers operate the same way when it comes to the church, expecting that more choices will be offered than can be taken. They are happy that the church has a Sunday evening service they will probably never attend, in sharp contrast with their parents who believe that one attends every scheduled meeting and event as an expression of church loyalty. The baby boomer likes different services not only at different hours but with various styles of music. They also like having several pastors; a solo pastorate seems quite restrictive.

Because so many baby boomers have learned that it is wrong to discriminate on the basis of race, gender, or age, they have extended the principle into a universal acceptance of just about everyone and everything. While this tolerance does not mean that boomers have no firm convictions, it does mean that they are highly accepting of persons with contrary convictions. The baby boomer who is a conservative Christian heterosexual opposed to nuclear disarmament may be fully accepting of a liberal agnostic homosexual who promotes nuclear disarmament. But this is more than tolerance; it has become a belief that what is right for me is right for me and what is right for you is right for you. Even absolutes begin to seem relative.

These views often set baby boomers at odds with their parents and grandparents. Yet in many instances the boomer attitude has pervaded and nearly persuaded even those older and younger than themselves.

It may be something of an over-simplification to explain this tolerance of diversity in terms of education, but there is no doubt that it is a major contributor. Cheryl Russell says:

> Nothing changes people so much as education. Education determines how they live, how they vote, what they buy, and what they believe. American society has become more diverse, and more accepting of diversity, because its members are more educated. This is why the baby boom forges new ways of life, and why there cannot be—no matter how much some people may want it—a return to the simple traditions of the past. Becoming educated makes life more complex because it turns black and white into shades of gray. Getting educated is like losing innocence—once lost, it is gone forever.[8]

McCall's magazine found this expressed in many ways in its 1988 readers' survey. Of the 18,000 respondents, 55% claimed to be "born again," and 41% said they attended church services every week. Yet most said they relied primarily on their own consciences rather than the traditions of their religions to make moral decisions. Less than 3% said they would go to a clergyman for guidance. A typical comment came from a Cincinnati woman who clearly stated that out-of-wedlock pregnancies and divorce are sin, but added that "the Bible is definitely against divorce, for instance, but sometimes you don't have a choice. God will forgive you . . . and He will give you the strength to go on with your life and be happy."

Comfortable with Change

Rapid and profound change has marked the twentieth century. To those from another era it would seem overwhelming. To those born after 1946 it is normal.

Historically the United States has a tradition of revolution. Our nation began with a revolution to bring about change, and we have valued change ever since. We boast the longest term of constitutional democracy in the world, and our Constitution is built on the premise that change is normal and good. Sys-

---

[8]Russell, op. cit., 40.

tematically we replace political leaders without coups or wars. This tradition has predisposed all Americans, regardless of generation, to cope with the changes of the century. However, the baby boomers are especially comfortable with continuous change.

John Parikhal, a Canadian executive and author who analyzed the lifestyles of 1,400 Americans between the ages of 38 and 42, says that "television created a push-button world for boomers. Changing channels gave people the chance to get control—and this leads them to expect control." While that doesn't seem to be much of an argument for coping with change, Parikhal adds, "Boomers were born into non-stop change. But they feel that they have control over change and so they feel comfortable with it."

Putting this together with the tolerance for diversity leads to an overall baby boomer perspective: "There are lots of choices. Some are good and some are bad. Everyone is free to pick their own. I can pick mine. I have control over my life by making my own choices."

This is not to say that boomers seek change for its own sake; but they accept and tolerate change more readily than others. As they move into positions of leadership and power, they will increasingly become the "change agents" for many institutions. And as this happens they will inevitably come into conflict with their parents, with older employees, and with present leaders.

Present leaders often try to guarantee the future of institutions by writing rules and regulations that will limit the freedom of future leaders to effect change. This trend is already apparent in churches and religious organizations where they attempt to control future orthodoxy through detailed doctrinal and procedural statements.

One Texas church had doctrinal standards written into the deed, stating that if the beliefs of the church were to change, the property was to be taken away from the leaders and given to another nearby "faithful" church.

This approach fails to recognize the responsibility of every generation to decide for itself. Orthodoxy cannot be guaranteed by a piece of paper but by the faith and convictions of the people themselves.

Some older leaders recognize that baby boomers will bring change they don't want, and they also recognize that they cannot maintain control with constitutions and by-laws. Their only alternative is to keep control of the leadership themselves. Sometimes this is done formally by not allowing younger leaders into positions of power. Sometimes it is done less formally by allowing the younger leaders into positions of leadership but keeping the power itself in the hands of the old-timers. In either case, it is a design for disaster. The organization will die with the old-timers.

Different Leadership Style

Managers from the pre-baby boom generation came to leadership in their organizations during an era of expanding economy and growing population when America was a power to be reckoned with around the world. Many industries, from banking to transportation to communication, were highly regulated, and most organizations were run from the top down. Leadership was challenging, but society was less complex and less competitive.

Today's emerging leaders are inheriting a very different set of working conditions. The United States no longer dominates most world markets, and we face fierce competition both home and abroad. Consumer and employee expectations are far greater.

On a personal level, many of these young leaders have been severe critics of the "establishment." They protested the Vietnam War and have continued to lobby for changes in politics and business. They are much more participative and democratic in their management style; they are less likely to make unilateral decisions at the top and more likely to be process oriented. They are much more attuned to employee needs for job satisfaction, women's rights, child care, and ongoing institutional change.

Author Jim Hillkirk adds three more specific characteristics:

1. *They favor a hands-on approach:* As managers they tend to communicate person-to-person. They like to touch and feel what's going on, and are less dependent upon financial figures. The boomers know the numbers, says George Stalk Jr., vice president of Boston Consulting Group, "but they don't lead with them."

2. *They're more media conscious:* Raised in the emerging global village, they're more knowledgeable—and concerned—about the news media. Vivid TV broadcasts from the Chicago convention, as protestors being driven back by club-wielding police chanted "The whole world is watching . . . ," proved just how powerful the medium can be.

3. *They're more entrepreneurial:* "We're far more willing to trust our instincts," says Mike Lorelli, 38, executive vice president for marketing of Pepsi-Cola Company.[9]

But are baby boomers really different? Some say no—that much is being made over nothing. Those born before World War II often changed their styles as they came into leadership positions, they say. One of the characteristics of a good leader is the ability to adapt to a changing environment. Others would say that today's older leaders also had their younger years of fighting the establishment and dreaming up new ideas.

Furthermore, many of America's institutions are led by powerful leaders who function as mentors, grooming their successors and leaving a strong imprint on them. Those unlike the present leaders are unlikely to be chosen for top positions. And if another argument is needed, they say, baby boomers age like everyone else and may tend to become more hierarchical and less participatory as they acquire the power and perquisites of top management.

All this is true. But one very large factor cannot be ignored.

---

[9] *"Boomers Are Moving into Boardrooms," USA Today* (31 August 1988): B:1–2.

Whether baby boomers are different or not may not really matter, because they *perceive* themselves as different. As one baby boomer executive put it: "We consciously think of ourselves as different than the people who came before us." This perception alone increases the sense of generational solidarity that will cause baby boomers to push older leaders out and attempt to run things differently.

Religion is not exempt from this leadership pattern. As baby boomers move into the boardrooms of business, they will also move into leadership positions within the church and religious organizations. Those that welcome them early will have a leading edge in reaching the vast number of other boomers. Those that are slow to open leadership to this generation will face constituency defection, internal revolution, or even institutional death. Baby boomers will become increasingly unwilling to take orders from pastors, elders, presidents, and boards that exclude them from the ownership and processes of the organization.

Different Motivating Values

Perhaps one of the greatest differences and one of the greatest sources of conflict between the older generation and the baby boomers is the matter of motivating values. Consider these comparisons discovered by surveys from the Harvard Business School's Advance Management Program.

Experience vs. Possessions
Baby boomers are not as motivated by materialism as their parents. Experiencing life (sports, trips, relationships) is more important than accumulating possessions. This makes baby boomers something of a mystery to the older managers who offer more pay and perks as motivation. They don't understand why the baby boomer may choose a lower level job with fewer work hours and less money.

Fun vs. Duty
This is similar to experience but particularly applicable to the workplace. Boomers want jobs they enjoy. When they don't

like the job, they are likely to quit. By contrast, their seniors are highly motivated by a sense of duty, whether they like the job or not.

Change vs. Stability

Older workers find security in stability; they want things to stay the way they are. Boomers are energized by variety, risk, and change.

Candor vs. Tact

Management expert Peter Drucker says that manners and politeness are the lubricants of business relationships. If this observation is true, boomers are at a disadvantage. They are accustomed to being candid and confrontal, while their parents prefer to be more tactful and indirect.

Professionalism vs. Journeymanism

The majority of baby boomers want to be considered professional at whatever they do. The old definition of professionals (doctors, lawyers, clergy) has been changed to include professional painters, professional truck drivers, professional mechanics, and so forth. As professionals, they want to be included in the decision-making process. Boomers consider their opinions valuable and bristle at managers who want to make the decisions by themselves.

The organization that wants to relate well to boomers will promote variety, treat everyone as a professional, value straight talk and truthfulness, encourage participation, minimize layers of management, and be sensitive to individual needs and relationships.

Seeking Meaning

Because of their unique experiences and characteristics, the baby boom generation is not well-equipped to understand and live life. As psychologist Martin E. P. Seligman points out, many baby boomers have lost confidence in government, their marriages and families have come apart, and they have little faith in God. All they have left is self, which he describes as "a very small and frail unit indeed." And, he adds, "the self is a very poor site for finding meaning."[10]

Previous generations turned to the family, the community, the government, the church, and God during difficult times. Many baby boomers have nowhere to turn.

The good news, according to Paul C. Light, is that "baby boomers appear to retain much of their commitment to finding a meaningful philosophy of life."[11] They are still searchers. They haven't given up.

It is not surprising that New Age ideas proliferate as baby boomers seek meaning for their lives. And for this reason they are also prime candidates for the Christian message. Many are already coming back to church. They want the best for their children, and that includes religious and moral values.

A word of caution, however: churches and Christian organizations will not effectively reach baby boomers with 1950 methods and programs. We must relate to boomers in terms of their distinctions and in response to their needs. Most won't just "show up" at a Sunday church service to hear the Gospel. They will be attracted by modern nursery facilities, excellent pre-schools, and attractive youth programs for their children. They will become open to the message of Jesus Christ during the transition times of their lives, such as divorce, remarriage, the birth of a child, unemployment, or the death of a parent. But that message will probably get to them through a divorce recovery workshop, an unemployment support group, or a workshop on grief rather than through a sermon.

The church that ministers to and accepts people where they are will be much more successful in reaching them with the truth and light they so sorely need.

Reaching a Generation

When I wrote an article about churches moving away from denominational names, a pre-baby boom reader sent a letter to the editor of the religious periodical reacting against what I had

---

[10]*Psychology Today* (October 1988): 55.
[11]Light, op. cit.

written. He said that what the baby boomers need to do is simply "Grow up!"

Well, they have grown up. But they haven't outgrown their characteristics, and telling them to grow up won't help. If they are to be reached, they must be reached where they are and as they are.

Baby boomers are starting back to church, especially the older ones born between 1945 and 1955. However, many traditional churches are not attracting them. Mainline denominations such as Lutherans, Presbyterians, Methodists, Episcopalians, and the United Church of Christ do not reflect the age distribution of the general population in their membership. They are well below the national average of persons under the age of 30. Church historian Martin Marty believes the mainline denominations may be moving to the sidelines of American religious life.

So where are the baby boomers going to enter the church? George Barna, himself a baby boomer and a California-based researcher, says that many attend three to five different churches at the same time. They go where they believe their needs are being met. "We are a generation that questions everything. Churches are going to have to deal with changes in the household. The family is different now. The population is growing through immigrations, not births," says Barna.

Some church leaders choose to change in order to evangelize and assimilate this generation. Others would rather have their institutions die with them. Still others want to reach a younger generation but struggle with principles: How do we stay true to the prophetic nature of the Bible and bend to meet every perceived need of the unchurched?

The fact is that it may not take theological bending as much as sociological adaptation. Lyle Schaller describes the type of church where baby boomers are going:

> While precise numbers are not available, my observations suggest that a disproportionately large number of the persons born after the close of World War II can be found in (a) "spirit filled" or self-identified charis-

matic churches, (b) new congregations organized since 1978, (c) churches that offer a strong adult Church education program (especially attractive to those born in the 1945–1960 period), (e) congregations with more than a thousand members and a specialized staff, (f) the theologically very conservative congregations, (g) churches that provide a Christian day school for children of members and (h) congregations that offer the stability and relational advantages provided by a long pastorate.[12]

For those churches and religious organizations that want to focus on reaching baby boomers for both survival and effectiveness, Schaller emphasizes the following things:

1. Preaching—"meaningful content in the sermons, and the communication skills of the preacher."

2. Vital Worship—"the carefully designed, fast-paced experience that touches people at a feeling level and evokes a sense of active involvement in worship, as contrasted to a spectator role."

3. Teaching Ministry—different from preaching, usually found in adult classes.

4. Strong Weekday Program.

5. Strong Ministry of Music.

6. Transformational Leadership—"The transformational leader is driven by a vision of a new tomorrow, wins supporters and followers for that vision, and transforms the congregation."

7. Change-Agent Skills—"Blending the old and the new requires a high level of competence in planned change and intentionality in program planning."

8. Challenge the People—high expectations of the people.

9. Continuity of Leadership—long tenure for the pastor.

10. Changing the Priorities—moving away from a one-to-one relationship with the pastor to relating to people in small groups.

---

[12]Lyle Schaller, "Whatever Happened to the Baby Boomers?" *MPL Journal* Vol. VI, No. 1, The Journal of the Minister's Personal Library (Waco, Texas: Word, Inc., 1985).

11. Advertise!
12. Athletics.
13. Choices—different services and multiple activities.
14. Parking—one off-street parking place for every two people attending the service with the highest attendance.
15. Facilities—higher quality reflected in buildings built after 1949.
16. Attractive Programs for Young Adults—rather than focusing on "singles."
17. Christian Day School[13].

Robert Bast draws up a similar list:

> The baby-boom generation has within it many people who are looking for:
> - a spiritual experience which brings them closer to God;
> - Biblical knowledge which relates to an opportunity to discuss life's concerns and faith questions;
> - help with family issues;
> - a sense of belonging;
> - an opportunity to serve in an important cause;
> - the development of deeper interpersonal relationships;
> - a chance for leadership.
>
> Churches that have demonstrated effectiveness in reaching the baby boom generation usually share a combination of common characteristics, which include:
> - a strong worship focus;
> - a meaningful educational program for all ages;
> - an orientation toward experience and practical action rather than a focus on intellectual and theoretical approaches;
> - a high degree of tolerance and an acceptance of diversity;
> - an emphasis on inclusion, with a particular con-

---

[13]*Net Results* (March 1989), 65–68.

cern to include women and newcomers in leadership;
- an informal style which is highly relational.[14]

To be sure, these ideas do not provide a magic formula for reaching baby boomers. Keeping a pastor who doesn't fit the church for a long tenure is not a good idea. Starting a Christian Day School in an area where parents have a high satisfaction with the public schools won't help either. Each ministry must learn the local culture and determine how best to reach the people. Nevertheless, these lists do incorporate many of the factors present in successfully reaching boomers.

Studies comparing different church groups indicate that the Southern Baptists are most effective in reaching those born from 1958 to 1965. Some of the reasons are similar. They are theologically conservative, aggressive in starting new churches (which are better able to adapt), strong in ministries to single adults, and offer large and structured Christian education programs for all ages.

The point is not to produce a checklist, but to be aware of the needs and interests of whoever is to be reached and to be willing to change the existing structures in a way that is responsible, responsive, and effective in reaching people.

These are not easy things to do. They require that we

1. decide who is to be reached
2. learn about those people
3. discover the most effective means of reaching them
4. change the church or other Christian organization accordingly.

In long-established institutions the last may be the hardest.

---

[14]Robert L. Bast, *Attracting New Members*, 29–30.

Chapter 6

Baby Busters: Generation in the Shadows

BY 1965 the pig had passed through the python and a whole new generation was born. The rules changed, the numbers decreased, and new distinctions began to form.

Those born after 1964 have lived in smaller families, attended schools with smaller classes, and often had their school closed or consolidated because there were too few students. Their teachers were older because only the tenured were not laid off. And because competition was not as great, it was easier to make a sports team, easier to be a cheerleader, easier to get into college, easier to win a scholarship, and easier to get a job.

It is too early to tell what shape this generation will take. (The first baby busters reached age 25 this year, 1990.) However, some very clear characteristics have already developed.

Most predominate is the fact that the baby bust generation has not had the same experiences as the boomers, nor do they share the same values. Women who fervently fought for women's rights are flabbergasted when their daughters either take those rights for granted or just don't agree. The Cold War fears of the baby boomers are neither understood nor appreciated by younger adults who have lived with more cordial and less confrontational international relations. The baby bust generation did not experience the Vietnam War and doesn't care about it. As one explained, the only anger over the Vietnam War occurred when the TV network preempted "Scooby Doo" cartoons to televise the signing of the peace papers.

Sense of Entitlement

The parents of the generation born since 1965 have often tried to give their children the best of everything. They have fewer children to provide for and often have two wage-earners to do the providing. Many baby busters have had things given to them—even forced on them—all of their lives. For them a normal life includes education, health care, modern inventions, and a comfortable future. They're entitled! Since they have faced less competition, they are often unacquainted with the realities of survival. In many ways they manifest the characteristics of young people who have grown up in a welfare state where there is little insecurity or fear about the basic uncertainties of life.

The shocker comes when baby busters graduate from school and move into the marketplace. Some don't even look for jobs; they expect jobs will come to them. They are not prepared to compete and are sometimes astounded at the seeming hostility and aggressiveness of the aging baby boomers who are ahead of them.

Lack of Deferred Gratification

Baby busters have never had to wait for the good things of life. Never have so many gotten so much so soon. Everything is in the present tense. Live for now. Don't worry about tomorrow. They are far removed from the Depression generation, who grew up with little except the promise of a hope for the future.

Rapid-fire TV ads all say "buy now." Parents with credit cards have been more than accomodating. Saving for college and "working my way through college" has been replaced by popular student loans that enable students to go to school first and pay later. Smaller families have meant fewer hand-me-downs and more new clothes for the baby busters. New products have appeared on the market at a faster pace, so that yesterday's tricycle has been replaced by skateboards, three-speeds, ten-speeds and now ATVs (All Terrain Vehicles), Jet Skis and 4 x 4s.

A generation has learned to get it now because it will be out of date tomorrow. Borrow, don't save. Pay later (or just let your parents pay for it). Comparatively few fix their dreams on tomorrow, do without today, and work hard to make tomorrow's dream come true.

Individualism and Isolation

Perhaps nothing symbolizes this generation more clearly than the way they listen to music. Their grandparents listened to the Big Bands and the radio. Their parents had "American Bandstand" and discos. The music may have been distinctively different, but they enjoyed it in similar fashions—in groups, at dances, or listening to the radio or records with friends. Baby busters get their music through headphones attached to CD and cassette players. It is a much more private, more isolated experience.

This sense of isolation has been compounded by their family situations. Many baby busters are children of divorce. They have grown up in unstable family relationships, single-parent homes, and blended families. When the unexpected crises of life come (and they surely do come, much to the surprise of many baby busters), they may not have a family to turn to for help.

As the baby bust generation moves through adolescence and into adulthood, they have been hit by another major cultural shift: the devaluation of children. For the first time in American history children are of significantly less economic and social value. While this devaluation is having a greater negative impact on younger children, as evidenced by the increase in child abuse, the older baby busters are also hurt by it.

When they hit the crises of early adulthood, they discover that their parents are glad they are gone and expect them to fend for themselves. Increasing numbers of parents who have heavily invested themselves and their resources in their children figure they have done all they are going to do and now want to focus on themselves.

To the older generations the baby busters seem self-centered and self-absorbed. They express little concern for the needs of others, the traditions of society, or for anything but themselves. Part of this is their age. Still young, many have not yet awakened to the greater world around them. But there is also a sense in which this narcissism is the product of their individualism and sense of entitlement. During their impressionable years they have been told how important they are, how they must value self-esteem, and how they are the fulfillment of their parents' dreams.

Postponed

Because they are finishing college later, marrying later, having children later, and entering the job market later, the baby busters are called "the postponed generation."[1] Some say that adolescence in America now lasts until age 28.

Nancy Smith, art director of *The Washington Post*, describes her generation well when she says that they are "grown-up yet still children, seeking experience without responsibility."

It is difficult to say why so many baby busters are so slow to grow up. Perhaps they fear an adult world with so many choices—they either want to try them all before deciding or are immobilized by so many to choose from. Later marriages may reflect their hurt over seeing so many failed marriages in their parents' generation. Later children are possible because of birth control and abortion, and necessary because both parents must work to afford to buy a house.

---

[1]Susan Littwin, *The Postponed Generation*, (New York: William Morrow and Company, Inc., 1986).

Unlike many other cultures, we do not have a clear line distinguishing childhood from adulthood. There is no rite of passage that ushers a boy into his manhood or a woman into her womanhood. Adolescence (13–18) has been the long American transition time. Baby busters are stretching the transition longer than before. It is not unusual to move in and out of the parents' house, switch majors, change jobs, postpone marriage and children. In other words, growing up and settling down is being put off as long as possible.

Fast-paced and Unfocused

Television has had an even greater effect on those born after 1960 than on the baby boomers. An entire generation has gotten used to instant coverage of one major crisis after another. However, their concern for issues is as unfocused, shallow, and fleeting as the evening news. Nancy Smith explains:

You guys had the burning causes. Yes, the issues are still there but our world is crammed with mini-crises, each with their 15 minutes of pop news fame. Issues flash so vividly and fade so quickly that we barely get attached to one when we have to psyche up for the next. Ironically, we go through crises so fast they have begun to repeat themselves. The environment and drugs were *the* issues when we were young, and now they're back for another installment. This time around they seem even more ominous: Crack is more addictive than mere heroin; the thinning ozone layer and the greenhouse effect are more threatening than simple pollution. Having been raised on TV, we're used to this— tuning in, tuning out. This news-bite sense of reality can have dangerous effects. It breeds an ever-shortening concern span: the length of time one has to care about an issue before it is replaced by another. Remember famine in Africa? Herpes? The nuclear freeze? AIDS has faded as an issue; drugs may fade, too. Concern span lasts as long as the image stays on the screen. End of episode.[2]

Of course, the same television coverage is seen by older generations, but the response is different. Many just ignore most of the issues and focus in on their chosen few. To them the baby busters seem to have no issues. Actually, they are concerned about certain matters, but for a much shorter period of time. They don't focus in on anything for very long. The result is a generation that doesn't seem to care, doesn't get involved with anything, and has even shorter commitments than the rest of the population.

Undecided and Indecisive

While the baby boomers may have grown up in a world of choice, people born after 1960 have faced the most overwhelming array of options of any generation ever. On the one hand, they seem to be overwhelmed. They cannot decide where to live, what to do, which to choose. They float from one thing to another—jobs, addresses, relationships, convictions. On the other hand, many feel they need to try everything before they decide. Whatever they buy or do, a better product or experience will come along next week or next year. Nothing is permanent. Leave your options open. In six months a better car, computer, or career will come on the market.

Nancy Smith says: "Decisiveness is certainly not our strongest characteristic . . . we reach for a goal, and once it's attained, we realize it has moved farther away."

Blurred Sex Roles

The baby busters may be called the first American unisex generation. Equality of the sexes has been taught to them since birth. Women can be airplane pilots and men can be nurses. Everyone wears jeans and sweatshirts. Girls who wear dresses

---

[2]*Networker* (September/October 1989): 15–16, reprinted from *The Washington Post*.

to school are by far the exception. And coed college dorms are the rule.

But there is more to the blurring of sex roles than jobs and jeans. This generation has also grown up having much closer contact between males and females, and the result is more of a friendship relationship than a mystery relationship. They know each other very well, but more like brothers and sisters. This close rapport is almost impossible for older generations to understand.

When a high school girl calls a high school boy on the phone and they talk long and often, parents assume there is a romance in progress. They simply don't believe their children when they say, "Oh, we're just friends." It is even more unbelievable when a group of young adult men and women share the same apartment and insist that there is nothing more than a platonic relationship between them. "Date" belongs to the vocabulary of their parents and grandparents. They just "do things together," often taking turns paying the check.

This blurring of the sexes causes some problems when a romantic and intimate relationship evolves. What are the roles in such a relationship? What's a man to do? What's a woman to do? Sexual relationships they can understand; but gender roles in marriage and family are often a mystery.

Comfortable with Contradictions

While the baby boomers are tolerant of diversity and comfortable with change, the baby busters are comfortable with contradictions. You can see it in their dress. Men wear business suits with earrings and ponytails. Women arrive at the office in suits and sneakers.

Their dress is symbolic of a generation that has a highly eclectic style. In fact, this is one of the reasons baby busters are so difficult to define and understand. What they have in common is that they have little in common. Their consistency is their inconsistency. They may hold contradictory beliefs, say contradictory things, and feel fine about it. Rather than trying to integrate all aspects of life and philosophy, they select their convictions a la carte. Life is like a cafeteria line where one can select a meal that includes caviar and pizza, Sausage McMuffin and shrimp scampi, apple pie and mustard sauce. In fact, many baby busters drink Coke or Pepsi for breakfast the way their elders drink orange juice or coffee. Needless to say, this diversity sounds neither sensible nor appetizing to older generations committed to consistency.

New Humor

Nancy Smith claims that their humor is one of the few qualities people notice about baby busters.

Frequently they don't get it. Our humor is deadpan, sometimes even vicious. It is Dan Quayle on a magazine cover with the headlines, "Mr. Stupid Goes to Washington"; it is "Heathers," a comedy about teen suicide. It's Penn and Teller, magicians who debunk magic's illusions. There's no limit to what's funny anymore— the mundane is hysterical, the serious is a joke. We are seriously unserious[3].

All this may sound sickeningly serious to older generations, but it is really a means of coping with the frustrations and absurdities of a complex and rapidly changing world. Unable to get control, the only apparent choices are despair and humor. Baby boomers get depressed; baby busters laugh.

Society and the church are just beginning to grapple with the challenge of effectively reaching the baby bust generation. And the overwhelming size of the baby boom generation will keep attention and resources focused on it for years to come. For this reason, the baby busters may continue to be comparatively neglected—forced to survive on their own as they ride the wake of the 77,000,000 baby boomers ahead of them. They tend to be a generation in the shadows.

---

[3]Ibid., 15–16.

Chapter 7

The Church and Change

IT WAS a snowy Sunday in London, and I was about to do something I had wanted to do for years. I was going to attend a worship service at the Metropolitan Tabernacle, site of the ministry of the famous Charles Haddon Spurgeon. When I was a child, my English mother had spoken of Spurgeon's ministry and read to us from his daily devotional book *Morning and Evening*.

Spurgeon was only nineteen years old when he was called to pastor the New Park Street Baptist Chapel in London. At the time, the building boasted a seating capacity of 1500, although attendance was less than 200. While young Spurgeon had had some modest success in a country church, he lacked college and seminary education and had not been formally ordained.

Within a few years as many as 23,000 had come to hear Spurgeon preach, and his sermons were being published weekly in English-language newspapers around the world. Nine years after he came to New Park Street, they built the large Metropolitan Tabernacle to accommodate the crowds, established a school to train pastors, and began a colportage (book distribution) business. Metropolitan Tabernacle became one of the most famous and significant religious institutions in nineteenth-century England.

Spurgeon's ministry was particularly known for successfully attracting people from every walk of life—from the poor of London to members of Parliament. During his thirty-eight years there, he built up a congregation of 6,000 and added 14,692 members to the church.

When I visited the Metropolitan Tabernacle on that Sunday in 1972, however, I counted eighty-seven worshipers present, and the speaker lamented how difficult it was to reach the people who lived in the immediate neighborhood. Much had changed in seventy-five years.

London had changed. The neighborhood had changed. Society and culture had changed. The world had changed. But this church had not kept up with the changes. And it is not alone.

America has its share of Metropolitan Tabernacles. Once great churches they are now barely surviving, mere shadows of their former selves. Mission organizations once on the cutting edge of world evangelization are now struggling for survival. Schools born out of vision and commitment now seem unfocused and lethargic. Then there are the institutions that have greater numerical success and secular stature than ever but have deviated widely from the beliefs of their founders. The former have not kept up with the times. The latter have changed with the times but abandoned their roots.

Some of this is just part of the normal life cycle of all institutions. Like plants and animals, they move from birth to death. In many instances the purpose of the institution is to serve one generation; it fulfills its purpose and closes down. Closing down takes courage and leadership, which many organizations lack. They keep going not to fulfill a purpose but to perpetuate an institution.

Barriers to Change

All institutions have a natural tendency to resist change, especially religious institutions. Such resistance is good; otherwise they would be like jellyfish, floating with every current. When institutions are unstable, anarchy reigns. Unfortunately, reluctance to change can also result in the creation of certain barriers. These must be overcome if religious organizations are to fulfill their God-given missions.

1. Focus on Institution Rather Than Purpose

The best organizations are purpose driven. They know *why* they exist. Wycliffe Bible Translators is an outstanding example.

Wycliffe was founded by Cameron Townsend for the specific purpose of providing a written Bible for each of the unwritten languages of the world. While Wycliffe has added airplanes, anthropology, printing, and other activities through the years, the original purpose still drives the organization. Everything else is subservient to the main mission.

Wycliffe has successfully resisted activities that, while good, do not fit its purpose. For example, Wycliffe members are not church planters, nor do they build hospitals, found colleges, or start denominations. Not that any of these endeavors are bad; but they would divert resources from Bible translation. In my opinion, Wycliffe would never have achieved its extraordinary success in translation if the organization had siphoned off energy, focus, and resources by branching into these other missionary works.

Their next great challenge will come when the last language is written and the final New Testament is dedicated. What will happen to Wycliffe Bible Translators then? Will the organization be dismantled? Or will it continue simply because there are so many members, employees, offices, donors, and programs to support? If the latter occurs, the focus will switch from purpose to institution. Unless, of course, the purpose is changed.

The March of Dimes faced this very challenge. The original purpose of the organization was to eliminate polio. Coin collection boxes with pictures of children in wheelchairs were placed beside cash registers and on lunch counters across

America. Millions of dollars were donated for research and treatment—much actually coming in the form of dimes. Then in the 1950s Dr. Jonas Salk produced the polio vaccine, and tens of millions were vaccinated. Next came Sabin's oral vaccine. Today polio has been virtually eliminated in the United States. The mission of the March of Dimes was fulfilled. So what happened to the organization? Rather than switch its focus from purpose to institution, the March of Dimes adopted a new purpose—fighting birth defects.

It could be argued that the purpose of churches and parachurch organizations will never be fulfilled until the world is won to Jesus Christ, and in a very broad sense this is true. But it misunderstands the practical and limited nature of each organization's individual purpose.

The purpose of the Sudan Interior Mission was to evangelize the people of Sudan. The purpose of the Moody Bible Institute was to train approved Christian workers. The purpose of World Relief Corporation was to provide relief and development to needy people in cooperation with churches.

Most churches begin with a sense of purpose, even if they lack a statement of purpose. They want to establish a place of worship for a certain group of people, or they want to reach an area evangelistically, or they want to represent a specific denomination. After a generation the purpose is either fulfilled or forgotten. But the building, staff, budget, missionaries, and members remain. Subtly, the purpose becomes to keep the institution going.

Institutional focus is an enemy of change because change will alter the institution and potentially put it at risk. Even the incorporation of newcomers threatens the status quo, so they are unconsciously rejected or severely limited in their influence. When the institution faces threats, the most common response is retrenchment and defensiveness, and resistance to change is strengthened.

Sometimes openness to change comes very late as an act of desperation. When institutional death is imminent, the holdouts at last become willing to change, but it is too late. Like the heart patient who rejects a transplant until he is in the final stages of congestive heart failure. By the time he changes his mind and is ready to act, he is too weak to survive the surgery.

2. *Socially Self-perpetuating*

Most churches and religious organizations attract and absorb people who are very much like those who are already members. Such self-perpetuating organizations can be very stable but very slow to change.

Basically there are two types of churches. One is the church that establishes systems to attract and incorporate persons who are different. The other is the church that institutionalizes self-perpetuation with strict rules to keep out anyone who is different. Both have risks. People who are different will change the church; people who are the same will keep the church from changing.

The desire for exclusiveness is often well-intentioned: leaders want to insure the purity of the group. Strict rules are established to control belief and behavior, and anyone who does not conform is kept out or kicked out. Unfortunately, such inbreeding makes change unlikely if not impossible. The institution is pure, but dead.

A common example of the socially self-perpetuating religious organization is the family church. There are thousands of such small churches, held together by family relationships. The sign outside may say "Welcome," but the visitor soon discovers that the only way to be fully assimilated and achieve influence is by marrying someone already in the church. Everybody is related.

Many ethnic churches and denominations began with the purpose of ministering to immigrants who did not speak English. This worked for the first generation, but by the second and third generations everyone spoke English. Self-perpetuation reigns, however, and now the intent is to keep out anyone who does not have Swedish or German or Dutch roots. Sometimes there appear to be obvious exceptions, such as the Swedish heritage church with a key lay leader named Smythe. But a little checking will probably show that his mother's maiden name was Johnson.

If not ethnic heritage, the common denominator may be race, income, education, a doctrinal idiosyncrasy, loyalty to the founder, commitment to a specific lifestyle, or just about anything else. Some of these are good and some are bad, but any self-perpetuation puts the brakes on change. These churches risk becoming closed systems that will discourage new ideas, feel self-sufficient, and define success as doing things the way they've always been done.

3. *Minority Rule*

Because America functions as a "one person—one vote" democracy, we generally think in terms of majority rule. Balancing this is a historic sensitivity for minority rights. Recent years have elevated the importance of minority rights as many have sought to protect persons of color, women (technically a majority but functionally a minority), the handicapped, and others. Much of the motivation for minority rights comes from biblical teaching and the Judeo-Christian ethic.

The democratic notion has permeated most of America's voluntary organizations. Rule by the majority is considered the norm. Even the Roman Catholic Church, which is a political monarchy, functions quite democratically in this country. Church constitutions and books of order specify rule by majority vote in most denominations (if not at the congregational level, then at the presbytery or synodical level).

The Bible teaches Christians to be concerned for others, to love one's enemies, and not to be a "stumbling block" to weaker believers. In many churches these are given an interesting application: that is, they allow a few dissenters to kill good ideas for change. For example, needed changes are permanently tabled in order to placate a single dissenter. By the time the dissenter dies, it is too late. Or what happens more often is that people who recognize the need for change give up in frustration and go elsewhere. This effectively freezes the status quo in place.

Just because the rules say that the majority decides doesn't mean things actually work that way. Often the majority go along in deference to the minority—a few who don't want change. This practice immobilizes many churches because there are almost always a few who resist every change.

Some churches and para-church organizations formalize minority rule by requiring unanimity in decisions. Usually this is done on the board level, where one dissenting vote stops change. The theological argument for this practice is based on the influence of the Holy Spirit in the mind of every believer and the assumption that the Spirit does not have a divided opinion. Therefore, the group should postpone decisions until the witness of the Spirit has convinced all to vote alike. Such systems work best when there is a strong dominant leader who convinces everyone to agree. That leader then becomes the source of change. Problems mushroom when that leader is gone but the system continues; then the power of veto is given to everyone in the decision-making body.

Required unanimity may function without being formalized. Some groups just work that way without ever saying so. The unwritten law is that the spiritual thing to do is to wait for the dissenter to come around. Under these circumstances, introducing change becomes very difficult.

4. Yesterday's Innovator

Some organizations have been blessed with powerful innovators who eventually become barriers to innovation.

Picture a leader who is young, intelligent, charismatic, innovative, and effective. He is either the founder or the reshaper of the organization. His signature is everywhere—on the buildings, the programs, the personnel, even the stationery design. He is extraordinarily gifted—the pastor who built the church, the president who made the college famous, the general director who put the mission on the map.

The trouble is that he was too good. He can't be matched, and nobody wants to try. His good ideas for yesterday have become the obsolete but unchangeable methods for today.

Peter Drucker says that the life of most good ideas is five to eight years. Consultants brought in to evaluate the situation may see that, but the people who had the ideas may not agree. They have a vested interest in the way things are.

To propose changes may be interpreted as disloyalty to the leader or as a denial of his original idea(s). When current innovators are labeled as traitors, many either shut up or quit. Either way, innovation is curtailed. All that is left is to perpetuate yesterday's innovations and implement yesterday's dreams. In a fast-changing world this is often a formula for failure.

5. *Not Inclined to Take Risks*

All change involves risk. The greater the change, the greater the risk. And to attempt to relate to modern Western culture without losing faith and integrity is high risk indeed.

Religious organizations resist risk, often for very normal and natural reasons:

- The church itself is rooted in twenty centuries of tradition.
- Young organizations tend to have younger leaders; older organizations tend to have older leaders. And churches and religious organizations tend to reflect the age of their leaders. People are less likely to take risks as they grow older; therefore, the older the church or the religious organization becomes, the less likely its leaders are to take risks. The longer a church or organization exists, the more likely it is that the positions of power will be held by non-risk takers.
- People tend to place a higher value on taking care of what they have rather than risking to get more and better. For most churches, protection of capital is more important than taking risks. This principle can be applied to money, programs, buildings, and people.
- People tend to place a higher value on stability than on innovation. What are the rewards for doing something

new and different? Often there are none. On the other hand, we give plaques, recognition Bibles, and additional responsibilities to those who persevere. We reward faithfulness, not changeableness.

Add up all these factors, and the sum is: be conservative.

6. *Unwillingness to Suffer Pain*

Pain is one of the universal side effects of change. Whether the change is bad or good, it is always accompanied by discomfort for some of the people in the organization. This experience is most often evident in personnel decisions.

Personnel need to be replaced, retooled, or retired if the church or organization is going to meet its God-given goals. Sometimes these people have served faithfully for a very long time: the forty-year Sunday school superintendent; the veteran senior missionary; the employee who started out as a bookkeeper for the founder and was promoted to comptroller; the pastor who is no longer effective, even though he hasn't done anything wrong.

Rather than suffer the pain of dealing with a personnel problem and rather than inflict pain on individuals, most churches and Christian organizations choose to live with the problem. Unfortunately, the resulting consequences can be devastating: ineffectiveness, incompetence, low morale, shrinking income, unfulfilled purpose.

But it isn't just personnel. Unwillingness to inflict pain can become pervasive. A church in Denver will not remodel a chapel into a needed classroom because the chapel was dedicated to a former pastor and the idea of remodeling is too painful to the old-timers. A mission organization cannot change its name, even though it is offensive to the Muslim people they are trying to reach, because a new name would be painful to longtime donors. A college refuses to repeal the rule requiring chapel attendance for fear of appearing liberal, although the area holds great potential for drawing older adult students who want night classes and can't come to morning chapels.

There is an old story about a physician who was the only surgeon available to operate on his son who was very ill. The father knew that the procedure would cause his son severe pain but it could save his life. He also knew that the young boy might not understand why his father was hurting him. Trying to explain, he told the boy: "I may hurt you, but I would never harm you." It is doubtful whether the little boy understood, but the father said it for himself as much as for his son. Then he did what he had to do and saved his son's life.

The church or para-church organization that needs to change will invariably suffer pain. But without pain there will be no change, and that may mean death. The best leaders are those willing to inflict the necessary hurt without doing harm.

Stability and Strength

Just as religious organizations have natural barriers to change, they also have natural tendencies toward stability and strength. These have helped to make the church one of the most enduring institutions in all of history.

1. Spiritual Values Lead the List

The church was founded by Jesus Christ, and He is still the head of the church. In theological terms this means the church is a "theocracy" (ruled by God) rather than a democracy (ruled by people). Its essential nature is supernatural, which distinguishes it from any other seemingly similar human institution.

The Bible is the rule for faith and practice. Christians acknowledge it as the supernatural source of inspired divine revelation. This factor distinguishes the church from other institutions based on human authority.

Doing the work of Jesus Christ is the ultimate mission of every organization and person bearing His name. We join with Him in His great ministry in this world. Theologically the church is "Body #2" of Jesus. "Body #1" was incarnated, born in Bethlehem, grew to sinless maturity, had all spiritual gifts, did the work of the Father on earth, died on the cross, rose from the dead, and ascended into heaven. When Jesus bodily ascended into heaven, the responsibility to physically represent and serve the Father on earth was transferred to the church, which is called "the body of Christ." The church has been endowed with all the gifts required to carry out the work of ministry. In a sense, we are Christ on earth.

These essentials *should not* and *cannot change.* The supernatural nature of the church has enabled it to survive severe persecution, heresy, poverty, and prosperity. While we may use the modern disciplines of sociology and management to be more effective, we dare not reduce the church to a merely human institution.

The balance and tension between revelation and relevance is what John Stott calls "two worlds." Liberal Christians have too often forsaken revelation for relevance, and conservative Christians have forsaken relevance for revelation. Neither is consistent with the incarnation of Jesus. The Son of God was divine and human. To be like Jesus we must not compromise any of the supernatural nor fail to be relevant to our world and generation.

In the commendable effort to be relevant we must be diligent students of people and trends. We must speak the language of our generation and constantly update our ministries if we are to be effective. Because the required effort is great, there may be a temptation to neglect the spiritual. To do so is to tear the heart out of Christian ministry and lower the work of the Gospel to something less than supernatural. The uncompromising balance must be maintained, forfeiting neither relevance nor revelation.

Ecclesiology (the doctrine of the church) has been a focus of study for twentieth century theologians. This realm of theology has strengthened scholarly understanding but has not always been adequately communicated on a popular level. In order to deal with the consumer mentality of our day, which feels little need for understanding such theology, prophetic voices must continually call the church back to being the church as defined in Scripture.

The theology of the church is in place but is not popularly understood. In contrast, the theology of the para-church is not in place. "Para-church" refers to organizations that are Christian but do not function as churches and do not call themselves churches. Examples include missions (The Evangelical Alliance Mission, Latin American Mission, WorldTeam, and many denominational mission societies); youth ministries (Youth for Christ, Young Life, InterVarsity Christian Fellowship, Campus Crusade for Christ); evangelistic organizations (Billy Graham, Luis Palau); discipleship organizations (Navigators, Churches Alive); and communication ministries (Christian Broadcasting Network, Back to the Bible Broadcast). We could also include counseling centers, camps, colleges and seminaries, and publishing houses.

Even within these organizations the lines of definition are not always clear. The Moody Bible Institute of Chicago is a school, a publishing house, a broadcasting network, and a conference center. Navigators sends missionaries around the world, but it also publishes books and magazines. Charles Swindoll, Robert Schuller, Charles Stanley, D. James Kennedy, and Ben Haden are pastors of local churches who have national radio or television programs.

Para-church organizations struggle with identity and must increase their efforts to define their role and responsibilities in the work of God. Since there is little developed para-church theology, such organizations lack some of the strength and stability of the historical church. Yet many have enjoyed higher visibility than the church.

2. Inverse Relationship of Size and Durability

There is an interesting and surprising inverse relationship between the size and the durability of American Protestant churches. Overall, the larger the church, the more fragile it is as an institution; and the smaller the church, the more durable it is. Because most churches are small, most churches endure.

Larger churches tend to be pastor-centered. Since pastors are subject to illness, moral failure, bad judgment, waning popularity, and death, the large church can tumble down with them. Parishioners, who do not have other loyalties (to denomination or to close personal friendships, for example), can be quick to leave the large church and go elsewhere. Banks are well aware of this risk and often require pastors to sign long-term contracts and "key man" life insurance policies before granting a church loan.

Smaller churches tend to be close-knit, often based on family relationships. When everyone in the church is related, pastors may come and go, the building may burn, and the finances may slip—but church members stay.

If small means stable, does that mean churches should shrink to survive? Not at all. The important issue is purpose. What has God called the church to do? Once that has been determined, the social realities of the church's size should be considered but not to the point of determining mission.

The connection between size and stability among para-church organizations is less clear. If they are leader-centered (like the Billy Graham Evangelistic Association), they are vulnerable at any size. If they are purpose-centered (like Wycliffe Bible Translators), they are more likely to be stable at any size.

Should we conclude, therefore, that Christian ministries should avoid popular leadership? Again, this is not the answer. Martin Luther was the personality God used for the Reformation, and today God uses selected leaders to fulfill the valid purposes of specific organizations. Full advantage should be taken of such strengths, but the weaknesses should not be ignored.

3. Customers Are Members

Unlike the typical business, churches incorporate their customers as members. The salespersons are also the customers, the candidates are the voters, the employers are the employees.

This web of relationships is a wonderful setup for a tight communication loop. The product and the customer cannot get too far removed from one another. If the customer doesn't like the way the organization is run, there is immediate opportunity for complaint through words, presence, and contributions (or lack thereof).

In many ways a church is like a family. There is a system in place with spoken and unspoken rules on how everyone is to relate and behave. These rules and roles have magnetic power to continue relationships and perpetuate the system.

Also, like families, churches may have systems that are unhealthy, and they may become dysfunctional. When this happens, it is usually necessary to bring in outside help to identify and address the dysfunction and move the whole system toward health. It is difficult if not impossible to change individuals without changing the system of which they are a part.

Such systems make churches strong and stable organizations. They keep people together and loyal. The system naturally stops defection and functions centripetally. Such is not the case with all social institutions—neighborhoods, Little League teams, and PTAs do not have the same strong social glue.

In a healthy church or para-church system, the structure processes and adapts to the feedback from the members. Change is highly valued, and stability comes from the positive values gained rather than from negative values feared. Healthy systems are inclusive rather than exclusive, accepting newcomers and assimilating them into the system.

Every system needs renewal. Those that are sick need to be healed. Those that are healthy will stay that way only through ongoing renewal.

Chapter 8

Spiritual Renewal and Sociological Renewal

ALTHOUGH HE TRIED not to let it show, Jonathan Platt was upset. Only five of the seventeen board members had showed up for the Crusade for Conquest board meeting. At Jonathan's urging, those present had finally decided to go ahead without a quorum. Further delay was impossible, they agreed. The issues being faced were too crucial. The survival of the organization was in question.

Over the last twenty years CFC had shrunk from a staff of nearly 100 to less than 30. Their budget of $875,000 was as large as ever but was underwritten more from bequests than from support by living donors.

The founder of CFC had been a visionary in the best sense, a dynamic World War II officer who later returned to Asia as a crusade evangelist. In 1950 his Japan crusades attracted thousands, many of whom professed conversion to Christ. Now he was in his eighties and served as minister-at-large for the organization. He was also an honorary member of the board, although he no longer attended board meetings.

Jonathan Platt, chairman of the board and son-in-law of the

founder, began the meeting with prayer: "Dear Father in heaven, we come to Thee in humble adoration. We seek Thy presence and power in this meeting, praying for Thee to bestow Thy gracious blessing on all that we here do. We are Thy faithful servants, called by Thee to win the lost of Asia to Thy precious Son. We beseech Thee to give us the zeal we once had. Raise up committed young men and women who do not consider the cost to fulfill Thy Great Commission. Enable us by Thy Spirit to be renewed in every way. Praying in Jesus' Name. Amen."

Peter Follister, general director of CFC and also a son-in-law of the founder, then gave the financial report. They had ended in the black the previous year because a generous bequest of over $100,000 had been received on December 30. Following the financial report, Follister reported the retirement of two long-term staff members, the lack of new applications to consider, and the proposal to temporarily close the Indonesian project.

A vigorous discussion of the ministries and needs of CFC followed. Proposals ranged from closing down ("which we cannot consider as long as our founder is still alive, because it would break his heart") to a call for three days of special prayer to revive the church and solve the problems CFC was facing.

CFC is a figment of my imagination. The burning issues within this hypothetical organization are not. They are concerns organizations and institutions face every year.

"Why is a once vigorous Christian organization facing such difficulty?" The board members would say it is a spiritual problem. Young people today are not willing to go to the mission field. They lack the commitment, the zeal for missions, and the love for God evidenced by their parents and grandparents. Coupled with that is the fact that materialistic American Christians are unwilling to support missions. And Asians are not as responsive to the Gospel because the people at home do not pray.

All these are spiritual explanations, leading to the conclusion that what is needed is spiritual renewal—prayer and fasting and repentance and fresh dedication.

Or could the issues be sociological? CFC has become a family-run operation at a time when religious dynasties are suspect. Also, crusade evangelism is not the effective method for the 1990s that it was for the 1950s. The very word "crusade" in CFC's name is repulsive to educated Indonesian Muslims, who immediately think of the anti-Islam Crusades of the Middle Ages. And finally, CFC's aging donor base is not being replaced by younger contributors.

Perhaps what CFC needs is not spiritual renewal, but a new name, reorganization, and more modern methods.

Apostolic Board Meeting

The relationship of the spiritual to the sociological is not a new issue. It was faced by the first-century Jerusalem church shortly after Pentecost. Acts 6 reports that they interrupted evangelism to address an ethnic conflict between Christian widows:

> In those days when the number of disciples was increasing, the Grecian Jews among them complained against the Hebraic Jews because their widows were being overlooked in the daily distribution of food. So the Twelve gathered all the disciples together and said, "It would not be right for us to neglect the ministry of the word of God in order to wait on tables. Brothers, choose seven men from among you who are known to be full of the Spirit and wisdom. We will turn this responsibility over to them and will give our attention to prayer and the ministry of the word."
>
> This proposal pleased the whole group. They chose Stephen, a man full of faith and of the Holy Spirit; also Philip, Procorus, Nicanor, Timon, Parmenas, and Nicolas from Antioch, a convert to Judaism. They presented these men to the apostles, who prayed and laid their hands on them.
>
> So the word of God spread. The number of disciples in Jerusalem increased rapidly, and a large number of priests became obedient to the faith (Acts 6:2–7).

The people involved in this story were all Jews who had become Christians. Yet within their community of faith they still had to deal with the reality of their Greek and Hebrew heritages. The accusation was that the Grecian widows weren't getting their fair share of the food, and the controversy was enough to break the spiritual solidarity and halt the progress of the church.

The apostles recognized this as primarily a sociological problem rather than a spiritual problem, and they solved it sociologically by appointing seven men to manage food distribution—all seven of whom had Greek names. In other words, they put Greeks in charge of the food so that the Greek widows would no longer be neglected.

The apostles did not ignore the spiritual dimension. They simply realized that the spiritual would suffer if the sociological was not handled, and they prayed over the seven managers when they were commissioned to their task. This early ability of church leaders to distinguish between the spiritual and the sociological and merge both into the solution has been a model for Christians ever since.

Spiritual Renewal

American Christianity has undergone significant spiritual renewal and expansion in the twentieth century. During the early decades, the battle between conservatives and liberals left the liberals largely victorious and the conservatives with a fortress mentality. By mid-century the liberals appeared to outnumber the conservatives; they controlled many influential institutions—from education to publishing—and held widespread intellectual credibility in the sympathetic climate of a growing scientific era.

In the second half of the century, however, many of these effects were reversed. As conservative Christians and churches grew in numbers, the liberals aged and decreased. While many factors contributed to this, Billy Graham leads the list.

Graham became the single most visible symbol of evangelical faith, bringing the Gospel message to millions through his crusades and broadcasts. The evangelical message became well known and clear to many Americans at a time when there was no single identifiable voice for liberal theology. If nothing else, Graham's prominence brought hope and encouragement to conservatives.

Crusade evangelism itself may have been a passing phenomenon. Research indicates that crusade evangelism is not particularly productive when the long-term results are compared to other evangelistic methods. But Graham's contribution extended far beyond his crusades. He used his fame and influence to found *Christianity Today* and to enable the establishment of numerous other evangelical ventures such as Fuller Theological Seminary, Gordon-Conwell Seminary, and the Lausanne Conference on World Evangelization.

Christianity Today began as a weak conservative competitor to the long-established and powerful *Christian Century* magazine. Today the positions are reversed. Fuller Theological Seminary is the largest independent seminary in the world. Conservatives hold a near monopoly on religious broadcasting worldwide, and they dominate religious publishing with thousands of titles and millions of books.

When Jimmy Carter sought the Democratic Party presidential nomination in 1976, he announced that he was "born again." What sounded odd to a secular press turned out to be the confession of over 25% of the American population. Presidents Reagan and Bush made similar statements of evangelical faith. Conservative Christians gained access to the White House and influence in public policy as never before.

At the same time, many evangelicals were climbing the socioeconomic ladder. Today they hold top positions in business and industry, have achieved prominence in the professions, and control huge amounts of money. All of this has given greatly increased financial resources to churches and other Christian organizations, and many of the largest and most influential religious institutions in America are evangelical in faith.

None of this is to say that prominence, power, numbers, and money add up to spiritual renewal. But they do indicate that the momentum has switched from the liberal to the conservative camp of American Christianity.

However, there are evidences of spiritual renewal quite independent of social and political power. Often these have been rooted in the Charismatic Renewal movement, although they go far beyond charismatic churches and theology.

1. *Worship*

In recent years a growing emphasis on worship as central to religious life became evident in several areas. Books about knowing God, divine attributes, and the God-centered life blossomed in popularity and even topped the best-seller lists. Devotional literature enjoyed increased popularity, along with personal devotions promoting worship of God and the "life of devotion."

Church music changed from experience-centered (popular from 1900–1970) to God-centered, and many groups sing only Scripture set to music or worship choruses during their worship services. In keeping with this trend, many churches now hire a "Minister of Worship and Music," rather than a "Music Director." Often this position is a higher staffing priority than the traditional youth pastor. And Christians transferring from one part of the country to another increasingly list "worship music" equal to or higher than preaching in the qualities they look for when searching for a new church.

In view of the importance of individualism and the prevalent self-centeredness in the culture, this evidence of spiritual renewal in the American church is something of a surprise. While Americans are historically religious, their religion has been very experiential in nature. The recent ground swell of emphasis on worship seems a strong expression of God-given spiritual renewal.

2. *Spiritual Gifts*

Until as late as the mid-1960s, spiritual gifts were either unknown or controversial. Outside of those in Pentecostal churches, few American Christians had any theology of spiritual gifts, and most of the sermons, books, and articles were polemical—either for or against speaking in tongues, healings, and miracles.

Then in the 1970s two major influences brought an emerging theology of spiritual gifts into prominence. On one side were the charismatic Christians; on the other were the "body life" proponents such as Ray Stedman. Churches and schools began teaching the concept that "every believer is a minister" who has a spiritual gift that is to be used for the glory of God, the growth of the church, and the expression of each believer's faith. Growing numbers of churches and believers were liberated from a structure that seemed to functionally presuppose that all gifts were held by the leader and no gifts were held by the followers. Today, there is widespread belief that gifts are broadly distributed by the Spirit to all Christians.

Spiritual gifts have been both a cause and an effect of spiritual renewal as ministry has been liberated from the clergy and increasingly become the privilege and responsibility of the laity.

3. Social Responsibility

Christians once had an active involvement in social issues corresponding to their faith. William Wilberforce helped bring about the abolition of slavery in the British Empire, and many American abolitionists were committed Christians.

Then in the early 1900s the "Social Gospel" became synonymous with liberal theology. Rather than be tarred with the liberal brush, most conservatives withdrew from social responsibility. The repeal of Prohibition and loss of ecclesiastical power triggered a general retrenchment of Christian activism in the public arena, giving rise to a fundamentalism that emphasized personal holiness and separatism. Unable to influence society, conservative Christians focused on those they could influence—themselves. Personal behavior codes that prohibited dancing, playing cards, attending the theater, smoking tobacco, and drinking alcoholic beverages took on great importance.

With the spiritual renewal of the second half of the century has come increased involvement in social issues. Today, evangelicals speak out vigorously against racial discrimination, economic injustice, political corruption, nuclear weapons, apartheid, pornography, domestic abuse, and other evils. The greatest social and moral issue to rally evangelicals has been abortion. With the support of their individual churches, Christians have formed organizations, held marches, picketed clinics, participated in political caucuses, elected political candidates, and fought lawsuits—all to stop abortion on demand.

Some may explain this increased social and political involvement as an expression of the power that comes from socioeconomic rise, and there is some truth to this. However, involvement based on moral and biblical conviction is much more than ordinary political activism. It is a further expression of spiritual renewal.

These and other evidences of spiritual renewal have given American evangelicalism an unprecedented power and popularity. But spiritual renewal is not enough if sociological barriers block the effective advance of Christianity.

Sociological Renewal

"All truth is God's truth," said Augustine. If this is true, then the fact that a church needs a bigger parking lot or a mission needs a new general director if they are to be effective is God's truth.

Changes in the community and culture must be identified and addressed if ongoing sociological renewal is to take place. A problem arises when leadership becomes entrenched in yesterday's social structures and practices.

Usually the founder of an organization is intuitively attuned to the society and trends of the times. The founder initiates the school, church, mission, or other organization in a way that is clear in mission and relevant in style. As the organization grows and matures, the leader increasingly services the organization and decreasingly relates to the outside. This is an unfortunate but natural setup for losing touch with the culture while amassing power inside the ministry. Eventually the ministry is unable to change because no one has the power to compete with the leader, and the leader continues to operate on the assumption that yesterday's society is the same as today's. What is even worse is the leader who is aware of the changes in society but sees those changes as threats to the organization. Then the leader is driven to preserve the organization against society rather than lead the organization to minister to society.

Consider the following examples of needed sociological renewal:

1. *Print vs. Image*

Prior to the late 1600s few Christians could read or had access to books. That is why statues, paintings, stained-glass windows, plays, and storytelling were so much a part of the church.

With the invention of the printing press, that began to change, and the basic means of communication was through the printed page. Today, most Christian organizations more than ten years old are print-oriented rather than image-oriented. In other words, they assume that the basic means of communication has not changed. But it has.

Decreasing numbers of Americans are readers. In fact, many cannot read. And many who can read choose to get their information through an audio-visual experience. Rather than read the newspaper, they watch the nightly news on television. Rather than read a book, they wait until it is made into a movie. Music presentations are multi-sensory (not just listening but seeing and smelling)—whether at a live concert with lasers or on MTV with sights that complement the sounds.

Reading promotes linear thinking—one idea logically follows another. Image-oriented persons are more inclined to think experientially. If they are to relate to a post-print generation, many churches and religious organizations will need a sociological renewal. Logic should not be abandoned, but image must be added.

2. Consumer-Responsive

Religion that assumes people will come and conform no longer works. That is the approach of a monopoly, such as some denominations once held in certain areas. There are few monopolies today. Choices abound. And the church that fails to be sensitive to the needs and desires of existing and potential "customers" will not get a hearing for its message.

A suburban Denver church hired an education consultant to help determine why Sunday school attendance was declining. In the course of his assessment, the consultant told the Christian Education committee about a study done for the Oakland, California, school system. The schools were plagued with restroom vandalism that had become very expensive. The study suggested that all restrooms be painted a certain shade of gray. The color was so depressingly uncomfortable that it shortened the time students stayed in the bathrooms. Shorter stays meant less vandalism. The consultant told the Christian Education committee that all of the classrooms in their building were painted that same shade of gray.

Ineffective Christian education and declining Sunday school attendance may not be the result of poor teaching or low commitment; they may be caused by something as simple as the color of the Sunday school rooms. In this case, doing some environmental study could have solved the problem.

Related to consumer responsiveness is the government by which a church or para-church organization operates. Some select self-perpetuating leadership, which excludes entry by newcomers or outsiders. Others are extremely open with a rotating system of leadership. However, the issue is not necessarily the structure itself. Any structure can be consumer-responsive and any structure can be unresponsive. The important thing is that the ethic of the system operate in a way that listens, responds, affirms, explains, and lets the people know they are heard.

3. *Folkways and Mores*

When ethnologists analyze a culture, they describe the rules of society in terms of what is allowed and what is forbidden. They distinguish between folkways (characteristics of a people—that is, the way they live) and mores (moral views that have the force of law through long use). For example, fishing early in the morning would be a folkway, whereas rules against incest would be mores.

Every Christian community has behavior rules, and it doesn't take long for the newcomer to learn what is acceptable and what is not. Rules range from length of hair to acceptance of adulterers. Each group also has its own folkways. There is no way of avoiding these social customs which often seem to appear from nowhere and then are repeated and reinforced until they are part of the group's personality.

Too often, however, folkways increase in importance until they take on the force of moral law. In some churches this has happened to such customs as men always wearing suits and women never wearing slacks, no clapping of hands in worship and no dating outside of the fellowship. When these folkways are challenged, the inflexible organization claims moral, if not biblical, authority in perpetuating the practice. This inflexibility soon makes the church or organization out-of-date and in need of sociological renewal.

The challenge is not to be rule-free, but to determine which rules are morally and biblically required rather than culturally convenient. Culturally convenient rules are inevitable but must be regularly updated; moral rules must be maintained and practiced, no matter what the current culture.

4. *Changing Evangelism's Starting Point*

First-century Christians had to deal with a totally pagan culture. The world they lived in and sought to evangelize had never heard of Jesus Christ and knew nothing about the Judeo-Christian God and religion.

For most of the twentieth century, American churches and

Christians have lived in the midst of a pre-evangelized culture. The majority of the people we have tried to evangelize have had some kind of religious background and were at least familiar with basic Christian ideas and vocabulary. Now the situation is rapidly changing. Millions of Americans have never been to church, never owned a Bible, and have no interest in nor sense of need for religion. Evangelism becomes extremely difficult when Christians in our pluralistic society limit their associations and activities to those who share their Christian beliefs and lifestyles. They don't have friends who are totally secular; they don't belong to the same clubs, share the same interests, or even converse with them at any length.

I once heard John Stott give an interesting analysis of his famous book *Basic Christianity*. He said that if he were writing it today, he would take a very different approach than he did three decades ago. The book grew out of a series of lectures he gave to university students who came to a church building and listened while Stott addressed them wearing his clerical robe. Today's students would never come to such a setting, and if they did, they would not have the religious background to understand what he said. Today, Stott says, he would have to begin with a more basic Christian message and present it in competition with other religions and philosophies.

If Christians and the church are to become effective in reaching modern pagans, we will need to go to them. In other words, we need to change the starting point of evangelism. We need to start where they are instead of where we are.

And when modern pagans do become Christians, they may not be able to make the sociological jump to the traditional churches and organizations now available. They will need new forms and expressions of the church which are not now imagined—churches for the previously unchurched.

These four points are only a few of the many renewal issues facing us today. The list also includes the shift from smaller minimum-service churches to larger full-service churches, the debate between churches with buildings and churches without walls, the major change from solo leadership to plural leadership, the move from exclusively male leadership to increasingly male-female leadership, the former dependence on many small donations to the growing dependence on a few large donations, the decline in neighborhood churches and the rise of regional churches, and the necessity of Sunday night church services to the demise of Sunday night services.

Para-church organizations also face sociological issues. In many cases, their time line for change is shorter than the time line for the church. One current issue is the difference in candidate concerns among missions.

In 1950 both the missions and the candidates were primarily concerned about divine call. If both were convinced that the individual or couple were called to missionary service, a ministry "marriage" was made and other details were worked out. By 1970 education was high on the list of qualifications. Baby boomers were better educated and more numerous, and missions wanted college and seminary graduates. The divine call was still important, but only a part of the equation. By 1990 candidates were asking missions about health insurance, retirement benefits, and education for yet-to-be-born children. Current candidates see themselves as consumers shopping for the best mission; old-timers wonder what happened to divine call and self-sacrifice. It may be both a spiritual and a sociological issue.

Older para-church organizations were born at a time when formal organization, visible structure, and stated membership were valued. Today, many ad hoc groups gather for a specific purpose and have little interest in a formal structure. They are more like task forces. They meet until the project is complete and then disband. Membership is irrelevant, visibility avoided, and incorporation unnecessary. This shift may call existing para-church organizations to pare down the structure into a leaner form that can move quickly and effectively.

A final example is a social change that threatens both the church and the para-church, and that is special interest groups. Today a large variety of highly vocal groups gather around single issues such as abortion, home schooling, women's rights, human rights, divorce, pornography, denominational promotion, and drug abuse. They reflect societal trends toward pluralism and individual choice. Often these groups insist that their agenda become the institution's agenda. If the institution agrees, it may alienate other significant parts of the constituency; if the institution resists, it will appear to be unresponsive to certain of its consumers.

Renewing

Renewal is not something we do at periodic intervals. The best organizations are always renewing. They are always going through a process of change in which they throw out the worst and retain the best. This sorting out process guarantees both stability and relevance.

Robert H. Waterman has studied and characterized many of America's top corporations in his book *The Renewal Factor: How the Best Get and Keep the Competitive Edge,* and many of his observations are applicable to the church and Christian organizations. Waterman describes renewing organizations as those not bound by rules and inflexibility. They set a general direction, and their managers set overall boundaries. After that they allow individual freedom and creativity. Structure is changed often and dramatically (he cites IBM for reorganizing every major unit in two-and-a-half years), and teamwork is encouraged. Focus is outward rather than inward. Renewing organizations accept the inevitability of change, says Waterman. They look for opportunities in crises and chaos. Causes drive them and unite them.

The renewing church or para-church organization must be bound by the cause of Jesus Christ but open to new ideas and changing structures. Distinction must be made between moral absolutes and cultural relatives. Yesterday's answers are not always appropriate for today's questions. Change and challenge should not be threatening but recognized as part of the process. Leaders must keep calling the organization and its people back to the Lordship of Jesus Christ and the standards of the Bible while challenging people to grow and innovate within the biblical boundaries. Fulfilling the mission is always more important than perpetuating traditions.

However, renewal in the 1990s also holds some dangers. The current generation is fixed in the present with little regard for the lessons and traditions of the past and minimal concern for the future. This fixation ignores the valuable contributions and warnings of earlier generations—risking repetition of past heresies and failures. Coupled with this risk is the privatization that has come with pluralism. In a world with so many options, Christian faith is construed by many to be a private preference rather than an absolute truth. If these secular values are allowed to take root and grow in the church, they will endanger the continuation of biblical standards of truth and practice.

Perhaps the greatest risk is a polarization among evangelicals. Into one camp will cluster the modern monastics—those holding to truth and tradition but isolated from society. In the other camp will cluster the modern post-Christian secularists—the sociologically relevant who are no longer truly Christian.

Both the challenges and opportunities are great. So is the range of responses.

Chapter 9

Range of Responses

AT 5:04 P.M. Pacific Daylight Time on Tuesday, October 17, 1989, the earth shook under the San Francisco Bay area. At Candlestick Park, the Oakland Athletics and San Francisco Giants were getting ready for the first pitch of the World Series.

Suddenly the lights flickered. Steel girders holding the upper deck began to sway, and pieces of concrete crumbled down. The announcer told spectators to leave. But when the initial quake ended its roll, fans began shouting, "Play Ball!"

Meanwhile, north of the ballpark in the Marina district of San Francisco, houses shifted off crumbling foundations and buildings collapsed. Gas lines exploded and fires spread.

Across the Bay in Oakland commuters were crushed to death as a mile-long section of Interstate 880 fell on rush-hour traffic.

By 5:05 P.M. the lives of thousands of people were altered forever because of powerful changes beneath the earth's crust. Simply saying "Play ball!" was not enough to counteract such cataclysmic forces.

When change occurs, there are many ways we can respond.

But one thing is impossible: we cannot stay the same. We cannot stop the clock of change. If we choose to respond by doing nothing, change will take control and impose its will.

Some persons and organizations try to control change; we call them proactive. They want to be the change agents; they want to initiate. Their numbers are few, their failures are many, and their impact can be enormous. Prophets, reformers, and missionaries are all proactive change agents. They see the way things are and envision the way things could be. They attempt to create a new order which no one else may want.

Most of us are reactive. We are not the shapers of society or the initiators of new orders. We are comparatively small currents in the tidal waves of change. What is most important to us is our commitment to a mission, and we effect change by fulfilling that mission in time, place, and context. If we are proactive at all, it is within the context of a group or organization.

Before we can tackle mission, however, we must determine the overall organizational response to change. Does the organization resist, ignore, or welcome change? The question is important not only in understanding what leaders are dealing with, but in determining whether the first change must be to develop an openness to change itself.

Most churches respond in one of the following ways. (The same range of responses also holds true for individuals and para-church organizations.)

Resistant Church

The Resistant Church is conservative in the purest definition of conservatism; that is, they want to keep things the way they are. In absolute terms, this church may fit anywhere along the theological gamut, from extreme fundamentalism to extreme liberalism.

Both the Old Amish and Roman Catholicism have characteristics of resistance. The Old Amish have concluded that their way of life is superior to that offered by modern changes. Consequently they have resisted modern dress, inventions, electricity, and education; and they have been surprisingly successful. In fact, they have even turned their resistance into business prosperity as tourists come to see their ways and buy their products. In a narrower sense Catholicism has resisted change with its insistence upon a celibate priesthood, adherence to ancient creeds, and governance by absolute hierarchy.

Resistance is not all bad. Many of the values and practices of modern society are not better than the old ways. Bigger is not always better—Peter Drucker comments that "the elephant is on the very edge of viability!" Those who resist change demonstrate courage, persistence, and security. It takes enormous institutional ego to stand alone when almost all others think you are wrong.

However, not all resistance is rooted in moral principle. Much resistance is the result of personal and institutional insecurity—a fear of change which results in isolation. In extreme cases, the leaders and members of the church refuse to acknowledge the changes occurring around them or develop their identity by criticizing the changes.

The resistant church is seldom an evangelistic church. Its primary market for growth lies with those who fear change and find comfort in isolation. More important, its institutional energy and resources are consumed by resistance and are unavailable for outreach. To successfully resist the powers of change requires enormous amounts of time, thought, communication, and money.

Yesterday's Church

Yesterday's Church keeps hoping that tomorrow will be 1954. It is not so much that they resist change as that they are nostalgic about yesterday.

This is the church that reminisces about a golden age and prays that it will return after the present parenthesis of change concludes. When the building is refurbished, it is in a style befitting the golden era. Music, liturgy, sermon topics, Bible version, literature, social activities, and management are as close to the old days as possible.

Yesterday's Church is the church that promotes denominationalism when it is perceived by many to be anachronistic. It is the Church of Christ that uses no musical instruments in an attempt to reconstruct the New Testament church in the twentieth century. It is the few Roman Catholic churches that still use Latin and the Tridentine Mass. And it is the church that continues the practice of altar calls with an all-Christian audience simply because they were so evangelistically successful in the 1950s.

Yesterday's Church has both advantages and disadvantages. On the positive side is the fact that because it is slow to change, this church is unlikely to be caught up in a passing and destructive fad. The major disadvantage is the cognitive dissonance inflicted on the people of the church. They are forced to live in a 1990s world all week and return to a 1950s world on Sundays. This church does not interpret life or equip its people for spirituality amid the stresses and pressures of modern society. This scenario is different from the Old Amish who attempt to keep all of life in a different era; at least with the latter there is consistency and integrity. Not so for the members of Yesterday's Church, which becomes an escape from everyday life rather than a resource for everyday living.

The reality is that next year will not be, can never be, 1954. There is no going back. Christianity cannot be constructed on fleeting nostalgia. Yesterday's Church will eventually die from the terminal disease of obsolescence.

Try Harder Church

"Don't work harder. Work smarter," is common advice given to everyone from employees to marriage partners, parents, schools, businesses, and churches.

The Try Harder Church genuinely wants to relate to the world today. It wants to win the world, not resist the world. Specific actions that seem more like yesterday than today are motivated by a desire to be Christ's church in more effective ways. The Try Harder Church is devoted to doing the same things better rather than trying to be better by doing different things.

Often this logic grows out of previous successes. If earlier efforts at house-to-house visitation, Sunday school contests, and prophetic conferences were successful, this church attempts to visit more homes, promote bigger contests, and get flashier prophecy teachers.

What they do not realize is that yesterday's methods can be counterproductive. In some suburban communities, house-to-house visitation is not welcome. It may even be forbidden or illegal in many apartment complexes and in certain communities. Sunday school contests to increase attendance and reach new people were very effective in the 1950s when the Sunday school was a primary entry point to the church. Today Sunday school may be the last program a newcomer joins. Entry points are special interest groups, weekday activities, Christmas Eve services, athletic programs, and Sunday worship services. The popular prophecy conferences of the 1960s and 1970s don't attract much interest in the 1990s. Instead, baby boomers are drawn to conferences teaching on marriage and the family.

It is painful to see well-meaning people give themselves and their resources to improving and promoting products few customers want. It is a little like selling prettier manual typewriters to a market that wants word processors.

Surrender Church

The Surrender Church is often more realistic and insightful than any of the above. It is a church that truly understands itself and its relationship to modern society; and on the basis of this understanding, it concludes that it cannot change, will not change, or is simply being swept away by change.

Ethnic churches lead the list of Surrender Churches. They originated to serve the needs of first generation immigrants who did not speak English, and many have been highly successful. The stress comes when a younger generation moves away from the language and heritage into English and mainstream American culture. If the ethnic church stays with its older people, it will die with them. If it changes to meet the needs of its young people, the old will be abandoned. Many choose to lose the young, continue to serve the old, and eventually close— having served one generation well and leaving the next generation to the care of others.

Changing neighborhoods also create Surrender Churches. White, middle-class communities give way to poorer minorities. Church members move to other neighborhoods or suburbs and drive back to a church that is isolated from its community. Current community members are unlikely to join a church that is not only a white and middle-class church, but is controlled by people who live fifteen miles away. Within a few years the church dies and the building passes to a new ministry that is tied to the immediate neighborhood.

There are other alternatives, of course. Rather than passively surrendering, these churches may become divine agents of Jesus Christ through renewed mission. It is easy to criticize those who surrender but difficult to continue the battle.

A very different type of surrender is that which gives in to cultural changes while abandoning spiritual absolutes. This tragedy happened in the eighteenth and nineteenth centuries when many New England Congregational churches abandoned Trinitarian theology and became Unitarian. The waves of change swept them off their theological foundations and they forsook orthodox Christianity. The same thing is possible today when churches simply surrender to the prevailing changes and accept New Age beliefs, popular immorality, theological universalism, self-centered programs for success, or any other non-Christian pressure.

Change is not only an opportunity for the church, it is also a test for the church. Change forces a continual evaluation of what is essential and what is not. Surrender may be appropriate and necessary when the changes are sociological nonessentials; surrender is inappropriate when Christian essentials are abandoned or altered.

Entrepreneurial Church

A popular and exciting response to late twentieth-century change is the emergence of the Entrepreneurial Church. These are much like the para-church organizations of earlier decades—founded by capable charismatic leaders who see a need and venture to meet it.

Church entrepreneurs may work within an established denomination, as did Robert Schuller. He and the Crystal Cathedral are prototypes for the recent movement.

Schuller started the Garden Grove Community Church under the auspices and in affiliation with the Reformed Church in America, the oldest continuous Protestant denomination in the United States. He went where there were few churches, polled hundreds of people on what they wanted, and began services in the non-threatening context of a drive-in theater. The church and pastor were pioneers in television ministry, and the church programs continue to focus on meeting the needs of the unchurched.

More typical of what is to come is Bill Hybels and the independent Willow Creek Community Church in South Barrington, Illinois. Hybels took an approach similar to Schuller. He asked people what they wanted or didn't want in a church, and out of their responses developed a program targeted to the unchurched—with practical and relevant sermons, drama, contemporary music, minimal mention of money, and many special programs for meeting specific needs.

Both Schuller and Hybels hold conferences to teach others how to develop the Entrepreneurial Church. Since few present or potential pastors can match the unique personalities and abilities of these two men, there will be few clones. However, the Entrepreneurial Church is not a passing fad.

The Entrepreneurial Church is started by one or a few motivated leaders who welcome the risk and adventure of something new. They are market-sensitive and attempt to take current trends and needs into consideration, using such up-to-date methodology as telemarketing, advertising, and high-tech communications. These churches seek to be highly relational. They plan to be big and offer full services from the start. Some have as many as 300 people, multiple services, and several pastors on their first Sunday. Entrepreneurial Churches are not usually affiliated with a denomination, although many denominations are attempting to start Entrepreneurial Churches.

Part of the attraction is the lack of tradition. There is no one to say, "We've never done it that way before." No creeds, no liturgy, no building, no budget, no history. Everything is new and fresh.

It is too soon to say how this movement will evolve. However, the early returns indicate that there may be cause for great concern. Many of the pastors in these churches are not theologically trained (one of the attractions is that anyone can lead an Entrepreneurial Church, so there is no barrier between laity and clergy). Often there is no connection to the past. While this seems to fit well with the mood of the 1990s, it has dangers as well. Lack of tradition, theological training, and denominational accountability increase the potential for doctrinal heresy and immorality. Because so many of the recent Entrepreneurial Churches have grown out of evangelical offshoots (people who have grown up in evangelical churches), the greater problems may not appear until the second generation.

Compounding the problem is the entrenched focus of seminaries that are unrelated to large churches and Entrepreneurial Churches. Many of the pastors of these churches did not attend seminary and are ambivalent if not hostile to seminary education. Meanwhile, the seminaries are training pastors for smaller established churches and scholars to teach in seminaries. Little is being done to bridge the gap between the two.

Renewing Church

The Renewing Church is established and stable and willing to capitalize on that stability in an ongoing quest for relevance. This church values both tradition and change and makes an effort to know theology and sociology, to be faithful to orthodoxy and practical to people.

Renewal is ongoing in this church. There is never a sense of satisfaction or arrival. Systems are set in place for regular evaluation and modification, and everything is open to question. Change for change's sake may actually be welcome in order to keep the organization flexible enough to change in the future when it is essential. People are polled and heard. The Renewing Church keeps an ear to God and an ear to the market.

In many ways the Renewing Church is the most promising of the alternatives but the most difficult to sustain. There is constant tension between the old and the new, yet this church accepts the tension as necessary. It would be far easier to fall into old patterns, surrender, or begin from scratch. Instead, the Renewing Church focuses its resources into knowing and fulfilling its purpose.

Almost all change comes through process. Multiple forces are at work for extended periods of time, leading to alteration from the inside and the outside. The process of courtship precedes marriage. The process of illness leads to death. The process of education leads to graduation.

It can be argued that even those point changes we think are unexpected are really part of a process as well. An earthquake happens at a point in time, but the pressures have been building for years. The fatal heart attack steals life in an instant, but it is the result of years of hidden heart disease. The processes were unknown, not absent.

One of the ways we can respond to change and even manage change is to see and understand the process. When we are aware of what is going on, we are far less likely to be taken by surprise. And we are in a much stronger position to impact the process in ways that will alter the outcome.

When churches or organizations begin confronting the reality of change, they become a part of the process of change; and they must begin with self-diagnosis. Consultants may help, but they are like physicians who diagnose and treat a patient only after the patient has felt a need and come for help. The initial effort begins with asking some important diagnostic questions.

Chapter 10

Diagnostic Questions

MOST PEOPLE don't go to a physician unless they are sick. Most men don't like to go even when they are sick! Women are better about getting regular checkups—which perhaps explains why they live longer.

Prior to any medical appointment, however, most of us go through some kind of personal self-diagnosis. Even if it is a regular checkup, we tend to evaluate in advance how we have been feeling, how our parts are working, and how we compare to the way we were at our last appointment.

Most churches and organizations function the same way. They don't seek help until they are sick. And even those healthy organizations that get annual checkups do some informal self-diagnosis before the auditor or outside consultant arrives.

All diagnoses depend on asking the right questions and getting honest answers. These evaluations pave the way for any needed changes. So if we want to do some church or organizational checkups, we need to begin by asking some diagnostic questions.

Why Do We Exist?

Aristotle taught that "Why?" is the most important question we can ask. It may also be the most difficult.

If we cannot adequately answer "Why?" we likely cannot answer Who? What? Where? When? or How? Yet many leaders just assume that the "Why?" has been answered and that the organization is far beyond such basics.

The simple way to test is to ask the question either informally or formally. Informally, you can bring the topic into conversation and ask a cross section of constituents: "Why do you think Old First Church exists? What is our reason for being here?"

If you prefer to do it formally, pass out a carefully worded questionnaire with a few simple questions. "To help our church, please take a moment to answer the following questions: (1) Why does our church exist? (2) What do you think our purpose is? (3) What do you think our purpose should be? Feel free to add any comments you think pertinent."

Responses will vary from insightful to ignorant. Some people are conceptual thinkers and others are not. Most will answer out of their personal experiences and need, but a few will answer out of a broader view of the organization and its mission.

Sometimes everyone agrees. The organization exists to "feed the poor people of our city," or "to evangelize Korean-speaking residents of the San Francisco Bay Area," or "to raise money for Christian broadcasting to West Africa." If the reason for existence is that clear and broadly owned, diagnosis is much easier. But such consensus is the exception rather than the rule.

The most common collective responses are: (1) No clear answer to "Why?"; or (2) A clear answer that is wrong.

If there is no clear answer, this does not automatically mean that the organization should cease to exist or that it is not doing good work. But it is much more difficult to be effective and to change when there is not a clear concept of purpose. If the organization is doing well and is generally healthy, the answer is there and just needs to be expressed. If the organization is doing poorly and is generally unhealthy, there may be no reason to exist. If there is no reason to exist, cosmetic changes will not solve the deeper problem. At that point the organization either needs to choose a purpose for being, close down, or be changed at random by some internal and external pressures.

Equally serious is a clear but wrong answer to "Why?" Take the case of a local church where most agree that the church exists "to win non-Christians and the unchurched to Jesus Christ," when the real reason for existence is to maintain a historic building. Here we have a form of self-deception that promotes ineffectiveness and inefficiency. It would be better to candidly agree on the real purpose and then set about doing a good job of keeping the old building going.

More important than how the broad constituency answers "Why?" is how the leaders answer. Their answers are the basis upon which they make the decisions that direct the organization; and if they are not agreed on why they are doing what they are doing, it is unlikely they will ever agree on what to do.

It is difficult to overestimate either the importance of answering "Why?" or the difficulty of answering it. Because of this tension, many choose to avoid it. Churches, para-church organizations, leaders, members, and employees who want ongoing renewal must rise to the challenge and answer "Why?"

Who's in Charge?

Each year in my Church Management class at Bethel Seminary in St. Paul, Minnesota, I assign students the project of determining the formal and informal organization of their churches. Part of the assignment is to draw the formal organization (the way the church claims to operate) and the informal organization (the way the church really operates).

The pictures of formal organizations are all quite predictable: boxes with lines connecting them. Some have the church board at the top with the membership at the bottom; some have the board at the bottom and the membership at the top. Some are quite complicated, with as many positions in the organization as people in the church; some are very simple and lean. Some include God; some don't.

The pictures of the informal organization vary greatly. I recall one that showed a church made up of two different groups—those coming before 1980 and those coming after 1980. All the power and positions belonged to the pre–1980 group.

Another was color-coded with green, blue, and red. Each represented a family in the church—green for Osmonds, blue for Fredericksons, red for Vaughns. Every position of influence was held by someone from one of these three families.

Then there was the church where there were four overlapping systems of special relationships: (1) friends of the former pastor; (2) those involved with the music program; (3) denominationalists; (4) persons interested in and working with the Christian Education program.

My favorite drawing of an informal organization featured a

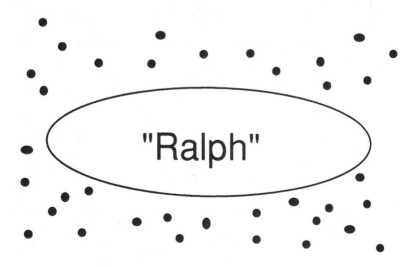

very large oval in the middle of the page surrounded by many dots. In the middle of the oval was the name "RALPH." No doubt about who was in charge or how that church operated! Even though there was a constitution and by-laws with elections and officers, nothing happened without Ralph's approval.

Identifying the informal organization and deciding who is in charge is an essential prerequisite to change. Here are some helpful questions:

1. *Who knows?*

Identify the person in the church to whom people go for and with information. Knowledge is power, and this person usually has great power. Sometimes it is the church secretary who doesn't even appear on the formal organizational chart.

If a stranger were to come to your church and want to ask

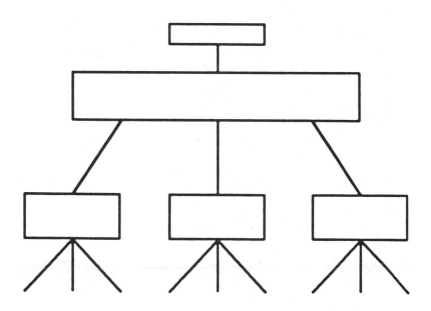

questions about the church's history, people, policies, operations, problems, and dreams, whom would you have them ask?

2. *Who is looked to spiritually?*

Once again, this person may not be the president or the pastor or the chairman. The person perceived as the spiritual leader may be someone completely different from those in formal positions.

When I was 24 years old, I became the senior pastor of a church of 200 in Colorado. According to the formal rules I was the spiritual leader of that church. The reality was a bit different. In our congregation was a godly old man, a retired Methodist minister, whom everyone called "Reverend Werner." Most of the church people knew him and sensed that he had a very close and powerful relationship with God. Reverend Werner was a man of prayer.

Suppose you were a member of that church in 1969, and one day you received a call from the hospital. A member of your family had been involved in a serious auto accident and you were wanted at the hospital immediately. The person was in surgery, where the doctors were trying to save his life. If you had time to call just one person in the church for special urgent prayer, whom would you call? Probably godly old Reverend Werner rather than your new 24-year-old pastor, right?—regardless of who the constitution said was supposed to be the spiritual leader of the church.

3. *How are newcomers brought into the organization?*

Growing organizations have "introducers" who meet newcomers and socially connect them to others. Even large organizations with thousands of people may have just a few introducers. These individuals are very important in the process of growth and change, for they continue to exert great influence even though they hold no formal position.

The introducer intuitively senses who is new. When a newcomer visits the church, the introducer gets acquainted, giving a warm welcome and answering introductory questions. Then the introducer takes the newcomer to others in the church and introduces them to each other. Once they are acquainted, the introducer usually abandons the newcomer to the others and starts looking for another newcomer. This process can take weeks or months. The introducer usually does not establish long-term relationships with new persons but makes sure that someone else does. This responsibility can give the introducer great organizational power—both in knowing and being known, and in serving as matchmaker for relationships.

Churches and social organizations that do not have an introducer are slow to grow. Visitors or newcomers are gone in six to twelve months because they are never able to penetrate the social barriers and become connected.

When Are the Best Days?

Everyone has certain periods of their lives that are better than others. Perhaps we look back at 1968 as "the good old days," or we look forward to 1998, thinking, "the best days are ahead." Some say, "This is the best time of my life right now." We may pity the elderly nursing home patient who has nothing to look forward to; or we share the excitement of the college senior who anticipates a new car for graduation, a June wedding, and a great new job starting in August.

Just as people have their different "days," so do organizations. Often there is a corporate sense of whether the best days were yesterday, are today, or will be tomorrow.

I have many acquaintances who have had long associations with one of America's great churches. They tell me about Sunday evening services in the 1940s and 1950s when people lined up a half hour in advance to make sure they could get seats. They talk about how good the music was and about the wonderful sermons. Only rarely do they say anything about the present, and they never say anything about the future.

When there is a corporate sense that the best days are gone forever, change for a better future is extremely difficult. Myths grow, making the past better than it actually was. The present can never match up or exceed these memories of former triumphs.

Those who think the best days are now will have a much more positive perspective, but may be disinclined to make changes for fear that today's successes will be at risk. The desire to continue the status quo can easily be an enemy of change. In situations where the present was achieved by changes, however, there is sometimes a positive attitude toward continued change.

Then there are those who think the best is yet to come. Their anticipation may be rooted in projections of present success or in a desire to leave the present and past behind. In either case, the atmosphere is conducive for instituting changes needed to deal with the future.

Which Way Do We Look? In or Out?

Organizational vision goes in one of two directions—either inward or outward. An organization's first priority is either serving itself or serving others.

Finding an organization's direction may not be easy. It may be necessary to ask many other questions: Was the organization named to please insiders or to attract outsiders? Is the budget weighted toward the needs of members or nonmembers? Are publications written for an internal reader or an external reader? Are schedules set for the convenience of the loyal insider or the convenience of the potential newcomer?

One vacation our family visited a large church for Sunday worship service. The weather was cold, and we were late. The parking lot attendant directed us to a parking place a considerable distance from the door. As we slipped and slid our way toward the building, I noticed a series of empty parking places near the front door. Each was marked "reserved" with the name of a staff member who obviously wasn't there. That church had chosen to save the best parking places for insiders, while requiring visitors to take what was left. It was one evidence of a church looking inside rather than outside.

Many businesses post mottos saying "The Customer Is

King," "We Work for the Customer," and "The Customer Is Always Right." All are evidences of an outward orientation.

The Chief Executive Officer of a major financial corporation has an annual objective to be away from his office 50% of his working hours. He insists on being out with the people, hearing what they have to say and serving them. That attitude is evidence of an outward look.

In the early 1980s, Wooddale Church in suburban Minneapolis undertook a major self-study. The leaders met, prayed, researched, and evaluated for over a year. They concluded that the church was inward rather than outward. Programs were geared to present parishioners and other believers. After this evaluation, the church made a major decision to change into an outward church. Nearly every program was reevaluated for its outreach potential, and the staff was reorganized. The church name and the membership requirements were altered. The existing building was sold, and the church moved nine miles and across three towns to a site better situated to reach out. None of these changes were made quickly or easily.

During the evaluation process, one of the most enlightening conversations took place in a public meeting where the proposed reorientation to outreach was presented. The particular point under discussion had to do with use of the church building—proposing that outsiders (especially non-Christians) be welcomed in every possible way so that they would feel at home and become familiar with Wooddale Church. It was a pre-evangelism strategy. The later implementation of the strategy opened the church facilities to the blood bank, Alcoholics Anonymous, birthing classes sponsored by a local hospital, city council meetings, corporate strategy sessions for nearby businesses, athletic events, concerts, and numerous other non-church events. During the public meeting when all this was proposed, a church member asked a practical question: "Will we allow these outsiders to smoke in the building?"

That one question brought the whole issue of inward versus outward into focus. People on the inside didn't want their building used by people who smoked. Yet some of the outsiders the church wanted to reach were smokers. Was the church willing to sacrifice its preferences for others? The answer given in the meeting was, "Yes. If permission to smoke will help us reach people for Jesus Christ, we'll allow it, because we want to remove every possible barrier for them." (As it turned out, the Minnesota Indoor Clean Air Act forbids smoking in public buildings, which made the question moot.)

Organizations focused inward are reluctant to change with society. They prefer to be self-serving. Organizations focused outward desire to change with society in order to reach people who are outsiders.

Are There Warning Signals?

Human bodies give many advance warning signs of disease. There is the sudden pain, the blurred vision, the upset stomach, the tiny lump.

Modern cars are designed to give advance warning of coming problems. A light comes on in the dash cluster indicating that the emission system needs to be serviced. The brakes emit an intermittent squeaking sound to warn that the pads will soon need to be replaced. Wear bars are built into the tires to encourage the owner to replace them before they become bald.

Organizations also have warning signals that alert us to problems before they become too serious. We are wise to heed these, for most difficulties are easier to remedy when they are small or relatively recent.

Management experts Peter Lorange and Robert T. Nelson list some of the "early warning signs" for large corporations, and these may be applied to churches and Christian organizations:[1]

- Excess personnel
- Tolerance of incompetence
- Cumbersome administrative procedures
- Disproportionate staff power

---

[1]"How to Recognize—and Avoid—Organizational Decline," Sloan Management Review (Spring 1987), 43–45.

- Replacement of substance with form
- Scarcity of goals and decision benchmarks
- Fear of embarrassment and conflict
- Loss of effective communication
- Outdated organizational structure

Specifically addressing the church, George Barna of the Barna Research Groups says that "the church in America has shown little forward progress over the past decade." Based on a five-year study during which he interviewed more than 100,000 Americans, Barna identified the "top illnesses" found in the church. They are summarized by Tom Winfield:[2]

- Pastors are ill-equipped by seminaries: Ministers are trained to preach, teach, and counsel and then are asked to run a [church] business.
- There's a lack of capable lay leaders to push the church forward. Few Christians feel adept at evangelism, and those who serve the church leave because they do not get the support they need.
- Churches spend five times as much money on buildings and maintenance as they do on promoting evangelism.
- Christians as a whole fail to hold each other accountable to Christian living.
- Christians haven't targeted special audiences with personalized messages (i.e., the homosexual community or abortion supporters).
- Schisms between fundamentalists, evangelicals, and charismatics; battles between mainliners and independents.

Each organization and individual should regularly be checking for warning signals of spiritual illness and organizational decline. There is no comprehensive checklist because the possibilities are infinite. However, the body of Christ can be regularly monitored just as our physical bodies can be reg-

---

[2]"Retailers Needed to Rescue Hurting Church," *Christian Retailing*, (September 15, 1989).

ularly monitored—we don't run through a self-check every morning, but we do watch out for the signs of cancer, evidences of heart disease, changes in weight, and so forth.

The unique danger to Christian organizations is that many of the warning signals are ignored because of misdirected applications of spiritual virtues. Needed accountability and confrontation are avoided because people fear that they will appear to be unloving, unforgiving, unkind, or impatient.

Jesus was loving, yet He confronted. The apostle Paul was unquestionably committed to the church, yet he frequently diagnosed and treated the spiritual and social illnesses of the first-century churches. In truth, failure to deal with the problems people and organizations face can be the most unloving action of all.

How Has Change Been Handled in the Past?

As important as change itself is the way change is handled. Look back over both the recent and not-so-recent past of the church or organization and list the major changes that have taken place. Some may be voluntary, like constructing a new building. Others may have been imposed, like the death of a beloved leader.

- Have such changes been accepted?
- Did it take a long time?
- Did people leave because of the changes?
- Were changes made in spite of opposition, or did a few negative votes stop the process?
- Would you consider the church or organization flexible and resilient?

Both persons and institutions tend to behave in the present and the future as they behaved in the past. If change came easily and naturally, it will come that way again. If change was resisted, or if it was painful and divisive in the past, it will probably be that way in the future. Of course, change should not be implemented because it is easy or avoided because it is difficult. Change should be implemented because it is right and because it fulfills the mission involved.

Chapter 11

Seeing Tomorrow Today

MAYFLOWER CHURCH had derived its name from the section of the affluent midwestern city where it was located, originally founded by pioneers from Boston. Colonial names and architecture abounded, including the church. The congregation reflected the community—older, stable, wealthy, traditional. The church had already plateaued when Pastor Jerald Coffman arrived. In fact, he was chosen because he was young, aggressive, and full of promise. Everyone hoped that he would attract younger families and lead the church into a bright new chapter.

Jerry had come from the staff of a much younger, more contemporary church. He had decided to leave there because he wanted to "run his own show" and implement many ideas he had heard about from other churches. Now he had the chance.

Shortly after arriving at Mayflower Church, he launched a series of Sunday evening sermons on AIDS, cocaine, child abuse, money management, and singleness. Rather than attract outsiders, he alienated insiders. Not that they were angry; they were just uninterested. Only the most loyal of the old-timers regularly attended Sunday evening church services anyway, and none of them knew anyone with AIDS or had ever seen cocaine. Their children were all raised. They had more accumulated wealth than the pastor would ever see. And almost all of them were married.

The next change focused on Sunday mornings. Jerry wanted to go to a contemporary style of service—no pulpit, no organ, no hymnals. Instead, he proposed drums, guitars, synthesizer, drama, and singing contemporary worship choruses with words projected on a screen. On the few Sundays the program was actually implemented, it made for an interesting sight. The old pipe organ was visible but silent. The colonial architecture seemed as shocked and stiff as the people in the pews. Few of them sang and none of them clapped.

The Reverend Jerald Coffman is no longer at Mayflower Church.

Deciding to change is only half the battle. We have to know what to change to.

Begin at the Beginning

Aristotle started with "Why?" and that is where anyone contemplating change should start. When we form a purpose or a mission statement, we are putting into words and formalizing our answer to "Why?"

Most churches and para-church organizations have a purpose statement. If they are incorporated, it is included in their constitution. The typical statement is longer than necessary and generally unknown to most of the people in the organization. For an existing organization with a purpose statement to begin at the beginning requires careful review. Even better is to "zero base," which means acting as if there were nothing at all in place.

Draw the leaders together and informally ask the "Why?" question. Write down the answers and begin to formulate a fresh statement. At first it will be long and cumbersome. Repeated revisions will streamline both wording and content. The final draft may be similar or even the same as the existing purpose statement, but going through the process is an essential part of any major change.

When the Evangelical Lutheran Church in America (ELCA) came into being from the merger of three Lutheran bodies, some individual churches chose not to join. One alternative to the merger was to join the American Association of Lutheran Churches (AALC). That was the choice of the newly formed Living Shepherd Lutheran Church in south Minneapolis. The original 27 members started a new church "that would meet the needs of people who believe in the infallible word of God and that Christ is an incarnation of God." This was a clear statement of purpose that served as a basis for specific goals the church targeted: (1) to expand to meet the needs of the community; (2) to give 5% of their offerings for a missions project in Africa; (3) to give 5% of their offerings to the AALC, which originally sponsored the church.

Wooddale Church in Eden Prairie, Minnesota, states that "the purpose of Wooddale Church is to honor God by bringing lives into harmony with Him and one another through fellowship, discipleship, and evangelism." To fulfill its mission, the church's organization is comprised of a Fellowship Board, a Discipleship Board, and an Evangelism Board. In the case of Wooddale Church, it was not a matter of drafting a new purpose statement, but of studying the existing statement, revising it somewhat, and then having it broadly owned by the church.

The purpose of the Evangelical Theological Society, organized in 1949, is "to foster conservative Biblical scholarship by providing a medium for the oral exchange and written expression of thought and research in the general field of the theological disciplines as centered in the Scriptures."

Christian organizations are not alone in having purpose statements. Most American businesses have them, and they often call them "mission statements," which sounds very Christian. Companies may spend hundreds of thousands of dollars and tens of thousands of hours developing, polishing, and promoting purpose statements. They are published in company magazines, publicized on building posters, and even incorporated in company advertisements. "Making a profit" may be part of the purpose, but seldom is that primary. The purpose of *The New York Times* is "to print all the news that's fit to print." The purpose of *Investment Vision,* a magazine of Fidelity Investments, is "to provide the best information on Fidelity's products and services." International Office Systems, Inc. puts it this way: "Best Product; Best Service; Best Price." Domino's Pizza's purpose is "to deliver."

Good purpose statements have certain characteristics:

1. They answer the question "Why?"
2. They are brief enough to be remembered.
3. They are long enough to be complete.
4. They are broad enough to be comprehensive for the organization.
5. They are understandable by both insiders and outsiders.

The process of developing or revising a purpose statement is a powerful catalyst for change in itself. The process takes the attention away from divisive specifics, provides a shared experience for all involved, and unites around the real reason for existence. It is a process that should take no shortcuts.

Learn the Market

Suggesting that Christians "learn the market" to be effective in their ministries sounds too secular for many; it smacks of Madison Avenue advertising. It also sounds exclusive to the point of being anti-Christian—because the Gospel of Jesus Christ is for everyone, not just a chosen segment of a market.

Surprisingly, however, the concepts of learning and reaching the market are deeply rooted in the New Testament. Jesus focused His ministry on Jews not Gentiles. Although He intended His Gospel to be universally offered, He began with a target market—the Jews of Israel.

Paul picked up on this in Romans 1:16 when he wrote: "I am not ashamed of the gospel, because it is the power of God for the salvation of everyone who believes: first for the Jew, then for the Gentile." He followed this priority in his missionary work, always starting with Jews in the synagogue and then moving on to the Gentiles.

First Corinthians 9:19–23 is a brilliant statement of this concept:

> Though I am free and belong to no man, I make myself a slave to everyone, to win as many as possible. To the Jews I became like a Jew, to win the Jews. To those under the law I became like one under the law (though I myself am not under the law), so as to win those under the law. To those not having the law I became like one not having the law (though I am not free from God's law but am under Christ's law), so as to win those not having the law. To the weak I became weak, to win the weak. I have become all things to all men so that by all possible means I might save some. I do all this for the sake of the gospel, that I may share in its blessings.

Paul practiced his teaching. When he went to Corinth where there was a synagogue, he started with the Jews and related to their Hebrew traditions and laws. However, when he went to Athens (Acts 17) he recognized a different market, and he addressed those on Mars Hill as a Greek, quoting from a pagan philosopher. Paul knew that different people had to be reached in different ways. Slaves were not like freemen; Jews were not like Gentiles.

The church or organization seeking to change, to be relevant to today's society, and to fulfill its purpose must learn its market. That requires getting to know people, understanding their languages and customs, and figuring out how to relate and communicate with them. There are internal markets and external markets. The people in the church may differ greatly from those outside.

Approach the markets of the church as a cultural anthropologist would approach the study of a foreign culture. Much information can be gathered at the library or local chamber of commerce. Determine the age, income, gender, marital status, religious preference, occupation, educational level, political affiliation, and other demographic data about those the church relates to. That's the easiest part, for much of what needs to be learned cannot be taken from census material. The next step requires lots of listening—going door-to-door with questions, reading the local newspaper, getting to know people around the church and community. How do they think? What do they like and dislike? What are their fears? What are their dreams? The successful analyst will be able to describe the target so well that those who hear will automatically say, "That's us he's talking about!"

Once you know the market, you must make some important decisions about whom to serve.

For example, it is impossible to serve a market that is not accessible. In an area with few singles, few blacks, few wealthy, or few elderly, those people are not readily accessible. Most churches must either target people like themselves or go where other people are. The more people are alike, the easier they are to reach; the more people are different, the harder they are to reach.

Some choose an internal market; they simply decide to serve the people they already have. In terms of access, that is the easiest job of all. However, does this address and fulfill the purpose of the organization?

When we target everyone, we usually hit no one. Therefore, it is better for a campus ministry to target college students but welcome university employees who are interested and responsive to the Gospel message. They may welcome all, but their main target is the college student. There is no doubt that a ministry for the young will have a different style than a ministry for the old, a ministry for the poor will differ from a ministry for the rich, a ministry for the educated will differ from a ministry for the uneducated, and a ministry for one of the minority races will differ from a ministry for whites.

Once the market is learned and targeted, the ministry must be molded to the market. If the market is ethnic Hmongs, then their language must be learned. If the market is elderly retirees, the church building should not have steps, and the church programs should not be held during evening hours. If the market is families with young children, resources must go into nursery facilities and programs for preschoolers. Changes must fit both the purpose and the market.

Decide the Nonnegotiables

Some sacrifices are too great to make. While Paul was willing to become all things to all men in order to save some, he was not willing to compromise the message of Jesus Christ. Because of his unwillingness to compromise his message, he was thrown out of synagogues and out of the temple.

The list of nonnegotiables may vary from time to time and place to place. In my opinion there are absolutes that should never be compromised at any time or place. But the list of absolute nonnegotiables should be short, and it includes the teachings of the Bible and the historic Christian faith. So the deity of Jesus Christ and the sanctity of marriage are nonnegotiable—we will not deny Jesus and we will not commit or condone adultery.

Some nonnegotiables may be practical rather than biblical, such as a historic church building. For example, the historic site and structure of Park Street Church on the Boston Common is probably a nonnegotiable for that congregation. The primary role of Billy Graham as evangelist is a nonnegotiable for the Billy Graham Evangelistic Association. Sometimes such nonnegotiables may be written into the purpose statement.

Unfortunately, there are often long lists of practical nonnegotiables that are not based on the Bible nor compatible with the purpose statement. A Bible distribution agency may have the purpose of "putting the written Word of God in the hands and hearts of unbelievers," but have a nonnegotiable commitment to the King James Version of the Bible. Since it is doubtful that many of today's readers can or will put antiquated words into their hearts, this nonnegotiable blocks the fulfillment of the organization's purpose. Most nonnegotiables are more subtle—such as spending money, doing things differently, style of leadership, and social rules.

From a purely practical point of view, those initiating

change should acknowledge what is negotiable and what is not. But from a biblical point of view, the nonnegotiables are directly from God and everything else is negotiable. In other words, we should be willing to change the rules and traditions if that will fulfill the mission.

Shaping the Vision

A few years ago I went to the ophthalmologist for my periodic eye examination. The technician seated me in a darkened room, removed my glasses, and asked if I could read the bottom line of the chart. I said I could and read, "A, Z, F, T, and it looks like a W." She wrote something down and started to leave the room. I asked her how I had done. "They're all numbers!" she said.

Obviously my vision isn't very good. I need correction to see reality—lenses that take away the distortions caused by astigmatism. On my own I can't tell a number from a letter.

And so it is with spiritual vision for God's work. Because of the distortion caused by sin, it is impossible for us to see God without the corrective work of divine grace that enables us to see as God sees. Only when we see God as He is are we able to see the church as it could be.

In Isaiah 6 the prophet speaks of a vision of God as He is and then a vision of Israel as it could be, from which we can draw a contemporary parallel: without a vision of God as He is, there is no vision of the church as it could be; without a vision of the church as it could be, the reality of our vision of God comes into question.

These visions for the avenues of God's work—in our case churches and Christian organizations—always have certain characteristics:

1. *Visions look to the future.*

It is something of an oxymoron to speak of a vision of the past. Visions by nature have to do with the future. The dictionary defines visions as the product of imagination. They are the sights and sounds of tomorrow.

The second half of Isaiah 6 describes God's vision of Israel seen through the imagination of the prophet. Isaiah saw the way things were not. In 740 B.C. Israel's cities did not lie in uninhabited ruins, nor were their houses deserted or their fields ruined and ravaged. Isaiah's vision was fixed on the way Israel would someday be.

2. Visions see the way things could be.

Robert Kennedy paraphrased George Bernard Shaw when he said, "There are some people who look at the way things are and ask 'Why?'; there are others who look at the way things could be and ask 'Why not?' "

Christians of vision spend little time bemoaning the rough realities of our world and asking "Why?" Instead, they look at the way things could be if the church were vital in prayer, devout in worship, informed in Scripture, aggressive in evangelism, close in fellowship, and zealous in missions—and they ask, "Why not?"

Nothing I've seen epitomizes the lack of vision more eloquently than the following urgent letter dated January 31, 1829:

To President Jackson:

The canal system of this country is being threatened by the spread of a new form of transportation known as "railroads." The federal government must preserve the canals for the following reasons:

One. If canal boats are supplanted by "railroads," serious unemployment will result. Captains, cooks, drivers, hostlers, repairmen and lock tenders will be left without means of livelihood, not to mention the numerous farmers now employed in growing hay for the horses.

Two. Boat builders would suffer and towline, whip and harness makers would be left destitute.

Three. Canal boats are absolutely essential to the

defense of the United States. In the event of the expected trouble with England, the Erie Canal would be the only means by which we could ever move the supplies so vital to waging modern war.

As you may well know, Mr. President, "railroad" carriages are pulled at the enormous speed of fifteen miles per hour by "engines" which, in addition to endangering life and limb of passengers, roar and snort their way through the countryside, setting fire to crops, scaring the livestock and frightening women and children. The Almighty certainly never intended that people should travel at such breakneck speed.

Martin Van Buren
Governor of New York

Let us not be ecclesiastical Martin Van Burens who see only the ways of the past and are blind to the possibilities of the future. Rather, let us recognize the reality of change. The "canals" of the past must be replaced with the "railroads" of the future if the church of the twenty-first century is to win its generation to Jesus Christ. Such an endeavor requires catching a glimpse of God's vision of the way things could be tomorrow and holding loosely to the way things used to be yesterday.

3. *Visions are in the eyes of the leaders.*

Whether in China's Tiananmen Square or at a local church board meeting, only a few leaders look to the future with genuine vision.

A few people—often just one person—imagines the way the organization could be. Not down to the last detail, of course, but the picture is complete enough to see a future very different from the present. Seeing such a vision is exciting and challenging, but rarely is it possible to enable everyone else to see that same vision. Imagination is not easily transferred.

Usually followers catch the vision through experience. They begin to understand only when they see the first tangible results of the vision coming true.

Look at the collapse of Soviet-style Communism in Eastern Europe. Only the boldest visionaries could have imagined the tearing down of the Berlin Wall, the reunification of Germany, democratic elections, and capitalist-style economies. But when a few tangible results showed up in Poland, people began to catch the vision. When greater changes occurred, millions caught the vision. In other words, as imagination turned into reality, the people bought into the vision for the future.

I had a similar experience as a pastor. I was serving a small church with little effective evangelism when a neighboring pastor told me about the Evangelism Explosion program. I read the book and began to envision many becoming Christians through evangelistic presentations in homes. No one else in the church shared the vision with me, but I tried the program and received a few positive responses. New Christians came to the church, and the vision became a small reality. Then I took some church members along on home visits and trained them. This elicited more results and more ownership of the vision. The wave spread until it was owned by scores of newly trained evangelists who week-by-week presented the Gospel and saw people coming to Christ and the church.

That is the way vision usually works: it begins in the eyes of the leader and grows through the experiences of the followers.

4. *Visions drive us to action.*

How could Isaiah sit and do nothing after he had seen a vision of God? How could he remain silent after he had seen what God wanted to do for Israel? The very character of vision causes action. Martin Luther envisioned a reformed church and was driven to bring about the Reformation. John Knox had a vision of an evangelized Scotland and set about winning his nation to Christ and the church. Mother Teresa had a vision of the poor of Calcutta dying with dignity, and so she picked them up and took them in and loved them in Jesus' name.

Francis Parkman was a nineteenth-century historian of French colonization in the New World. He wrote many books, including *Pioneers of France in the New World*. In his introduction to the latter, he explained the difference between the British approach and the French approach. In New England everyone worked hard in his or her little area, doing the best to succeed in a small circle. In New France there was a gigantic ambition to grasp the continent. The French failed; the English succeeded.

Of course there is nothing wrong with having a vision of winning the whole world. But the only way it is going to happen is if each individual turns that vision into action in his or her own sphere of influence.

Counting the Cost

Change seldom comes cheap. It has a price tag of time, money, and people.

Recently Charleen and I considered adding a room to our house in order to provide additional living and entertaining space for family and friends. What seemed to best fit our family and entertainment needs was a new family room added to the back of the house. Our vision was an addition about 15 x 20 feet (the size was set by one nonnegotiable: no damage to the large maple tree in the backyard) with many large windows, a fireplace, and double doors on the south side, leading to a deck for outside entertaining and barbecuing in the warmer months of the year.

Next came cost. We did some checking and were surprised how expensive such an addition would be. We looked at our savings and our borrowing potential and concluded that we could afford the addition, but the cost would limit other parts of our lives. Paying for the addition would mean fewer family vacations; it would use up money we had saved for our children's college education; and it would mean fewer discretionary dollars for such things as spontaneous family outings to McDonalds. We counted the cost—not just in dollars—and the cost was too high.

But there was also a cost for not making the change. Family gatherings are more crowded in our present living space, and our entertaining must be limited to smaller groups. We do not have a deck for backyard entertaining nor the comfort and glow of a fireplace. Either way, there is a cost.

When organizations implement changes, the costs are higher. Reshaping a church takes many hours of hard work, accompanied by the inevitable misunderstandings and emotional pain. Some members feel alienated and forced to leave. Longtime friendships may be severed. Hiring staff, printing literature, adding programs, sending missionaries, aiding the poor, buying a van, or tearing down a building can cost thousands or even millions of dollars. It is not just a matter of where the money for change will come from, but where it will not go—because deciding to spend it in one area means it is not available for another.

Total costs can never be fully anticipated. Money is measurable and is therefore the easiest to estimate; but time and emotions and relationships are difficult to quantify. Yet we must try. In Luke 14:25–35, Jesus encouraged us to count the cost of becoming disciples.

Sometimes the cost becomes clear very quickly. In order to change the para-church organization so it can fulfill its mission and relate to its market, the longtime leader may have to be replaced. The cost may be high in hurt feelings, misunderstanding, and divided loyalties.

Sometimes there are hidden costs that don't show up until the change is underway. That has happened to churches that have chosen to leave their denominations, only to later be sued by the denomination and lose the church property.

I am not suggesting that a "cold calculation" be made in which changes are counted in terms of bodies and bucks. Rather, I am suggesting that there be an up-front recognition that changes usually come with a high price tag. Preparation for paying the price is a valuable part of the process.

In the construction trade there is an interesting unwritten understanding among remodeling contractors. When they bid on a remodeling job and they are bidding against contractors who usually do only new construction, the remodelers almost always come in with much higher bids. Remodelers know from experience that it can be much more expensive to change something already built than to build something from scratch. Remodeling requires tearing down before building up, remodeling means encountering pipes and wires no one knew were there, and remodeling must work around existing structures.

For similar reasons many entrepreneurs would rather start a new church or organization than try to change one that has been around for a long time. However, the reality is that in most instances people must deal with what is already in place.

A central axiom of church growth theorists is that "for a church to grow, it must want to grow and be willing to pay the price." Likewise, in order to change, a church must choose to change and be willing to pay the price.

In his inaugural address on January 20, 1961, President John Kennedy said:

All this will not be finished in the first one hundred days. Nor will it be finished in the first one thousand days, nor in the life of this administration, not even perhaps in our lifetime on this planet. But let us begin.

The choice to change is not change itself. The actual change takes a long time—sometimes more than a lifetime. But let us begin.

agree on the way to do it. Aristotle put it differently but communicated the same idea: "Once a man understands an idea, he can identify with it, acknowledge it and make it his own."

Decide Before the Decision

In implementing change, beware of focusing on the formal organization and ignoring the informal organization. While the formal rules should be followed, the informal organization is by far more important.

In some situations the formal organization votes for a budget that the informal organization doesn't own. As a result, people don't give the money to underwrite the budget. This is a common occurrence in denominations. Leaders follow *Roberts' Rules of Order* to the letter, and the proposed budget is voted in. But the rank and file of the denomination doesn't agree, doesn't know, or doesn't care. Then when income doesn't match budget and an "approved" budget isn't met, the leaders can't understand why.

The better way to make any group decision is to thoroughly involve the informal organization until it owns the decision; then hold the formal vote as a ratification of a decision that has already been made. It may take longer and be more work up front, but in the long run it means less work because there is no reactive "damage control."

One of the results of this approach is that no formal vote ever fails. It can't fail because the decision has already been made.

This is really what happens with a wedding. A couple want to get married. They come to the pastor and have multiple meetings that include interviewing, testing, and counseling. Everyone agrees that there should be a marriage before the wedding is posted on the church calendar and announced to family and friends. The day before the wedding everyone involved rehearses every step and word. At the rehearsal the pastor says, "You are sure you still want to go through with this, aren't you?" and the man and the woman both say yes. They even practice saying "I do" and reciting their vows.

What happens at the wedding? There are no surprises. The bride and groom answer all the pastor's questions in the affirmative because the decision has already been made. The prior processing guarantees the outcome.

If this type of time, respect, and processing were given to all major decisions in churches and Christian organizations, change could become smoother and less painful.

Share Experiences

Shared experiences are a powerful force in uniting people for change. In fact, in some ways the sharing itself is more important than the actual experience.

1. *Praying Together*

Praying together lowers the walls of resistance in relationships. It is very difficult to dislike persons with whom you have prayed frequently—especially if the prayer has dealt with the pressing issues in each person's private life. It is amazing how well board members can discuss and handle decisions when they have been in the practice of praying for each others' jobs, health, and families.

For me it was a profound spiritual experience when the chairman of the elder board passed out sheets of paper listing all the elders and their family members. He even provided an extra wallet-size copy for those elders who travel frequently. Then he went around the table asking each one, "Do you promise to pray daily for each elder, spouse, and child?" Every elder said, "Yes, I promise." Those promises were renewed each year as we shared successes and failures, promotions and unemployment, life and death.

2. *Serving in Ministry*

Serving God together is a totally different experience from making decisions in a businesslike setting. I have seen close personal relationships grow between persons who have team-taught a Sunday school class, planned an evangelistic event, visited the sick, or raised money for a project. In many healthy Christian organizations there are firm expectations that leaders must minister before they can govern.

3. *Visiting Other Sites*

In 1981 when Wooddale Church was considering relocation, we researched about four dozen churches across America that had relocated in the previous decade. A telephone survey of each provided enough basic data to select twelve for on-site visits. Four of us spent two weeks traveling from Wisconsin to Washington to Arizona. While enormous amounts of helpful data and ideas were gathered, it was even more beneficial just to experience solidarity with others who had been where we hoped to go.

At the conclusion of every visit we asked, "What would you do differently if you had it to do over again?" Every church gave the same answer: "We would buy more land." As a result, the team of four returned home to Minnesota recommending that Wooddale Church double the amount of land we planned to purchase. This turned out to be a wise decision rooted in a shared experience.

Taking several days each year to visit other churches, headquarters, offices, or ministries will not only give many ideas for change but will also grant permission to change. Seeing how others have handled similar issues relaxes opposition to change and encourages people to believe, "We can do that too!"

4. *Sharing Crisis*

Nothing will bind people together like a crisis. Unlike prayer, ministry, and visits, crisis cannot be planned, but it invariably comes to us all. And when it does, the experiences shared during that time are not only good for the individuals, but good for the church.

When fire destroyed the old downtown building of a historic New Hampshire church, it was an unwelcome crisis. But the bad was used for good when the people rose to the challenge: a young, inexperienced pastor demonstrated leadership no one had seen before; a new building was established on a new site; and the church entered a chapter of unprecedented opportunity. Those who lived through that crisis and came out of it triumphant were united in ways that routine experiences seldom provide.

It doesn't have to be a fire, of course. The crisis may be financial, moral, organizational, or personal. It may be the death of a pastor's child, the retirement of a founding president, or the opportunity to merge with another organization. Every crisis provides an opportunity to unite people for change.

5. *Sharing Activities*

The list of possible shared experiences is long and varied: retreats for fun, growth, or planning; traveling together on vacations; eating out together, either on a picnic or at a restaurant; tutoring immigrants or the underprivileged; joining a political action group; hearing a lecture and evaluating it; watching the same TV program and discussing it afterward.

Even reading the same books can provide an important shared experience. It provides a common vocabulary, a common information base, and an opportunity to discuss issues independent of specific proposals for the organization. I've experienced this with such diverse titles as *Spiritual Leadership* by Oswald Sanders; *In Search of Excellence* by Peters and Waterman; *Imitation of Christ* by Thomas a Kempis; *Your Church Can Grow* by C. Peter Wagner; and *It's a Different World* by Lyle Schaller.

When I am asked the secret of the teamwork on our staff, my answer usually surprises the inquirer. I say that we meet together as a staff twice every day. At first some think I am joking, but it is true. At ten o'clock every morning and at three o'clock every afternoon our entire staff joins together for a beverage break. Every staff member who is in the building is expected to come, and all appointments are scheduled around these two fifteen-minute breaks if at all possible. Visitors are always welcome, and usually some are present. Some days we tell lots of jokes; some days we share serious matters and pray. Some days we just catch up on everybody's vacations, cars, children, and health; some days we talk business. This regular time together builds a foundation of common knowledge and shared experiences that enables us to handle hard work, big decisions, and major changes almost routinely.

Raise the Predictability of Success

Some small but significant approaches help increase the predictability of success in effecting change.

1. *Start with dissatisfaction.*

A satisfied need never motivates anyone. A totally satisfied person won't even get out of bed in the morning because there is no need!

Only when people are discontented with the way things are will they want change. Therefore, change agents are always on the lookout for dissatisfaction and how it can be mobilized for positive change. Fortunately, there is plenty of dissatisfaction around to work with.

In a mission the dissatisfaction may be with the number of missionaries, or with the shortage of support, or with the number of converts. People want things changed.

In a church dissatisfaction can center on the youth program, or the sermons, or the music, or some other person or program. Rather than seeing this as an irritating source of criticism, see it as a potential entry point for change.

Seek to state the dissatisfaction in ways that reflect understanding of the other person's position. Then suggest ways that the person can be satisfied through involvement, contribution, or some other change.

2. *Begin with a winner.*

Some changes are much more likely to succeed than others. Take the contrasting examples of two churches desiring to motivate their people to invite visitors to church.

Church #1 planned a series of "Fifth Sunday Night" concerts and encouraged the congregation to invite visitors. The chances of success were poor because most visitors would rather come on a Sunday morning than on a Sunday evening. Also, several of the fifth Sundays fell on holiday weekends when attendance is normally low and many people are either out of town or have special commitments at home.

Church #2 planned their visitor events for Easter Sunday morning and for the Christmas Eve service—the two church services that are the mostly likely to draw visitors.

The first church missed out because they started with a loser, while the second church virtually guaranteed success by starting with a winner.

3. *Start small.*

Introduce change a piece at a time. Let people get used to the first change before pushing them on to a second. But don't allow so much time between changes that the momentum is lost.

For example, if the major desired change is to move the organizational headquarters from California to North Carolina and there is a lot of resistance, consider first opening a branch office in North Carolina. Staff the new office with enthusiastic employees who will send back positive reports about the possibilities rather than the problems with a relocation.

4. *Build ownership.*

Orders from the boss or the board rarely build ownership. Ownership comes when individuals feel they are an integral part of the change.

Every opportunity for input, every plan for participation,

every sharing of information builds the sense of individual ownership.

Individualized missionary support is a good example. Donors who contribute to the General Fund may not feel like owners of the ministry. When they are sending their money for a specific missionary doing a specific ministry, their sense of ownership will be much greater.

Encourage and Accept Accountability

Regularly calling the organization and all of its members to accountability encourages an atmosphere that can support change. No one is permitted to be an outside critic; everyone participates and reports.

This begins with the leadership. The board and leaders should have annual goals that are known to everyone. Comments and suggestions should be welcomed. One year later at the annual meeting those same leaders should report their performance on each goal. Their failures and successes should be announced and explained.

Followers have a right to hold their leaders accountable. Peter Drucker says that the one thing every soldier has a right to is competent command.

The same standard applies to everyone in the organization. Membership means responsibility as well as privilege. Church members should be expected to attend, give, minister, and participate. When accountability runs through an organization, it brings structure and discipline that strengthens the organization for the rigors of ongoing renewal and change. It also keeps the organization in a constant cycle of self-evaluation.

Change Can Be Chaotic

Our fast-changing world often creates chaos—whether in the political upheavals of Europe and Asia or the roller-coaster changes in the stock market and interest rates.

Recently I sat in a meeting with some financial experts. I was out of their league when it came to vocabulary and concepts about money, but I did understand what they said about predicting interest rates. After a few comments about articles in *The Wall Street Journal* and some quotes from leading economists, they all agreed that *nobody* knows whether interest rates are going to go up or down. The only sure prediction is that there is no sure prediction.

Unpredictability, constant change, chaos—they have all become the standard of the times. Instead of fearing them and fighting them, we must begin to use them for good, like the winds and tides that sailors use to get to their destination.

In the introduction to *Thriving on Chaos*, author Tom Peters makes this positive and helpful statement:

> To thrive "amidst" chaos means to cope or come to grips with it, to succeed in spite of it. But that is too reactive an approach, and misses the point. The true objective is to take the chaos as given and learn to thrive *on* it. The winners of tomorrow will deal *proactively* with chaos, will look at the chaos per se as the source of market advantage, not as a problem to be got around. Chaos and uncertainty are (will be) market opportunities for the wise; capitalizing on fleeting market anomalies will be the successful business's greatest accomplishment.

Christians have the best of all. We serve a sovereign God who is unchanging and unchangeable. There is nothing chaotic about Him. He is the same today as He was yesterday and as He will be tomorrow. Yet we must also face the enormous opportunities and responsibilities that come with our circumstances.

Christianity has often flourished during changing and chaotic times. The fall of Jerusalem in A.D. 70 was the height of both change and chaos in Palestine and Judaism, and it was the springboard for the spread of Christianity and the evangelization of the Mediterranean world.

Who will step forward and take the risk of being a change agent? Who will be the leader who leads?

Chapter 13

Leaders Who Lead

AT THE BEGINNING of the twentieth century, many considered John Mott the leading Christian statesman in the world. Mott was a Methodist layman who had founded the Christian Student Movement. He was a compelling leader who persuaded many young men and women to Christian faith and missionary service.

Mott was offered the U.S. ambassadorship to China, but he refused it. He was asked to be Woodrow Wilson's successor as president of Princeton University, but he declined. He was offered the position of Secretary of State of the United States, but he said no. Why did Mott turn down every one of these important and prestigious positions? Because he wanted to continue his role in Christian service.

Mott defined a leader as "one who knows the road, who can keep ahead, and who can pull others after him." A simpler way of saying this is that "a leader is one who leads."

King Josiah was such a leader. When he came to the throne of Judah at age eight, the nation was essentially pagan. Heathen altars stood on the high hills, and the people offered incense to false gods. Yahweh was forgotten, the law was lost, the temple was closed, and the Passover was distant history. When Josiah died thirty-one years later, the face of the nation had changed. The pagan altars had been demolished, the covenant had been renewed, the law was read, the temple was open, the priests were faithful, the Passover was observed, and Yahweh was worshiped. Josiah was a leader who led.

Leaders who lead are quite unlike those who merely implement consensus. Consensus implementors determine the mind of the followers and help them do what they want done. It is sort of a mail-order-catalog approach to leadership, where the people choose what they want and get it whether it fits or not.

Lyle Schaller explains the difference, distinguishing them as transactional leaders and transformational leaders:

> "You want to know why this congregation changed from growing older and smaller to growing younger and larger?" asked a longtime member from a church that had made that change. "I'll tell you. Our new minister is a real leader and that has made all the difference in the world!"
>
> A majority of ministers appear to accept the role of a transactional leader or coach or enabler, who focuses on people in general and on individuals in particular. This is appropriate and highly popular in smaller congregations who love gregarious, articulate, person-centered, extroverted, and caring transactional leadership.
>
> By contrast, the transformational leader is driven by a vision of a new tomorrow, wins supporters and followers for that vision, and transforms the congregation. The change from growing older and smaller to growing younger and larger represents radical change, discontinuity, and requires a new set of priorities. It is a transformation. This often is reflected in the comment of the old-timer who observes, "It sure is different here from when I joined thirty years ago."[1]

---

[1]Lyle Schaller, *Net Results* (March 1989), 66.

The transformational leader who leads has many characteristics, but let's consider four that relate directly to change in churches and Christian organizations.

Transformational Leaders Stay Close to the Action

A frightened young recruit was in his first battle. As the fighting heated up and fear gripped his soul, he began a one-man retreat, running away from the battle line. The private had covered quite a bit of ground before he was stopped by an officer with a service revolver who threatened him with a summary court marital and execution. "Captain, please don't shoot. Please give me another chance," cried the trembling young man. "All right, private, I'll give you another chance," said the officer. "But it's 'Colonel' not 'Captain.' " To which the young soldier replied, "I'm sorry, sir. I didn't realize I was that far back!"

Not all armies keep their officers in the back. Following the British blunders during the Boer War, a young journalist named Winston Churchill wrote up his recommendations for change, which included placing high-ranking officers on the front lines. While his ideas were not adopted by the British military, Churchill followed his own advice. He personally viewed all of the French battles of World War I, and he frequently showed up in dangerous places in London when he was the Prime Minister during World War II. In 1948 his suggestions were adopted by the new state of Israel, and the modern Israeli army is one of the most formidable fighting forces in history. Even generals fight at the front.

This principle applies to medicine as well as the military. William James Mayo (1861–1939) and Charles Horace Mayo (1865–1939) founded the famous Mayo Clinic in Rochester, Minnesota, which has become one of the largest medical centers in the world. When the Mayo brothers, both surgeons, were in charge of the clinic, they had an interesting rule. Any surgeon who had not operated for three weeks must return to the operating room as an assistant before operating again. It didn't matter if the physician was chief of surgery, three weeks away meant he wasn't close to the action.

Leaders who lead stay close to the action. The best educators still teach. The best preachers spend time in counseling so that they understand those who are hurting.

One of my former responsibilities was approving expense account reports for staff members. One staff pastor turned in expense reports every other month and always for only ten or twenty dollars. After noting this pattern, I met with him and explained that this was unacceptable and must change. Such low expenses indicated that he wasn't taking people out to lunch nor was he driving to where the people were. To fulfill his role as a pastor-leader meant that he had to get out more.

If leaders allow themselves to become isolated in the problems and perspectives of leadership, they lose touch with those whom they claim to lead. This is a subtle thing that can easily happen. When they lose contact with people and society, they no longer understand and they become ineffective.

The leader who leads must understand the culture, which comes from reading, listening, visiting, and observing. The leader learns to understand people by going where they work, visiting in their homes, sharing their joys and sorrows, and sticking close enough that leadership is not divorced from followership.

Transformational Leaders Get Authority from Followers

Many studies and theories hypothesize about the source of leadership authority. Traditional wisdom says that authority comes from above—that it is "handed down." This is the teaching and practice of the Roman Catholic Church and most military organizations. They believe that authority flows from the Pope down to the people, or from the generals down through the ranks to the fighting men and women. There is truth to this approach, although even it depends on the parishioner or soldier accepting the theory in order for it to work.

Modern leadership theory sees authority flowing upward from followers to leaders.

Bring in a coach the team doesn't respect, or an officer the troops don't believe in, or a pastor the people don't know, and you'll quickly see that authority must be conferred. People will follow only those whom they choose to follow.

At this point it is important to distinguish between authority and power. Power is holding a gun to a person's head or withholding a paycheck from an employee. Power forces others to obey, even against their wills. Authority is earned. Authority is freely given. Authority is people listening to and acting on the words of a leader because they choose to and want to. Authority is trust and confidence. Not understanding the difference and assuming authority that has not been given is a certain route to disaster in a church or an organization.

When I first came to Wooddale Church in 1977, I had very little authority. I was 32 years old, and I was following a successful pastorate that had lasted 19 years. It took years of being with people, loving them, serving them, marrying them, burying them, and otherwise pastoring them before they chose to give me authority as their leader. For example, in 1977 I switched one item in the established order of worship (moving the invocation after the opening hymn instead of before), and the response was so strong and the objections so many that I restored the old order. It was obvious that I didn't have authority from the people, even for such a simple change. Eight years later the church changed its name, sold its building, moved to a large property in another town, and spent millions of dollars on the construction of a new church building. The difference? The people had given me authority to lead.

Too often would-be leaders fail because they do not understand this principle. They think that a college degree, a call from a church, and a title on the door give them the authority to lead. But it's not that easy.

Jesus demonstrated this truth. He "made himself nothing, taking the very nature of a servant, being made in human likeness" (Phil. 2:7). At the Incarnation, Jesus did not come into our world wearing a name tag, "King of kings and Lord of lords." His disciples followed Him because they chose to give Him the authority to lead. He did not use His power to impose leadership.

The *Clergy Journal* used to have a monthly column called "Dear Amicus," sort of the pastoral equivalent of "Dear Abby." One issue included a letter from a disgruntled senior pastor. At a recent church function there had been a shortage of chairs. Some who needed seats had asked him to fetch some chairs to set up in the back of the room. He did it, but he was outraged, writing, "Don't they know who I am? The senior pastor of a large metropolitan church should not be expected to carry chairs like a common custodian!" Amicus wrote back: "Dear Disgusted, have you forgotten that we are followers of Him who came not to be served but to serve?"

Christian leaders should adopt the leadership style of Jesus, who washed His disciples' feet. Interestingly, the "old style" of Jesus is as up-to-date as modern leadership theory.

Transformational Leaders Excel Amid Adversity

Over the past twenty years I have been involved in numerous searches to fill high-level leadership positions in churches and Christian organizations. As a result I have heard many explanations of candidates' successes and failures in leadership. Often the reports explain that the candidate left a particular position because of problems: "The people didn't want the church to grow"; "The faculty was hard to get along with"; "Financial resources just weren't there"; or "A lot of personal problems got mixed in with ministry issues." All of these problems were very real. It is a tough world, and Christian organizations and their leaders are not exempt. However, the best of leaders often excel amid adversity.

In *Megatrends* John Naisbitt says that the great presidents of the United States were Washington, Lincoln, and Roosevelt; between them most of the presidents were "What's his name?" These three presidents were great because their times were the worst. They led the nation through the Revolutionary War, the Civil War, and World War II. Adversity is when we need great leaders. We can muddle through the good times all by ourselves, but we need great leaders to get us through the tough times.

Alistair Cooke's *Six Men* includes the biographies of some of the famous people he has known. One of these was Edward VIII, the king of England who abdicated his throne to marry the American divorcee he loved. The last line of Cooke's biography sums up the Duke of Windsor's life, saying, "He was at his very best when times were good."

What a terrible indictment! It is no wonder he was not a great leader. He would have been worthless in the dark days of Nazi invasion that followed soon after his abdication.

Great leaders who lead excel amid adversity. So don't resent the tough times. Don't mark off the days until the problems will be over. It is in hardship that we learn endurance. It is in difficulty that we become strong. And it is in adversity that we have our greatest opportunities to lead.

Adversity is often the window of opportunity for change. Few people or organizations want to change when there is prosperity and peace. Major changes are often precipitated by necessity.

Have you ever watched a high school basketball game between schools with longstanding rivalries? It comes down to the last few seconds of the game. The home team has the ball but is losing by one point. There is time for one last shot. If it goes in, there will be ecstasy. If it misses, there will be agony. Isn't it amazing how many times the ball can be passed in the final seconds of such a game? That's because few players want to be holding the ball when the buzzer sounds and the determining shot must be made. It's at that moment that leadership comes to the fore. The leader wants the ball. He'll take the risk. He'll make the shot. He'll excel amid adversity.

Transformational Leaders Take the Initiative

When I go to a physician, I have certain expectations:

1. I expect a physician to take the initiative in diagnosing and prescribing. Yes, I want them to ask me questions and listen carefully to my symptoms, but I don't want a doctor who tries to determine my opinion and then implements it.

2. I expect a physician to do what is in my best interest.

They dare not be motivated by fee or fame. Their motivation must be to make me healthy or keep me healthy.

3. I expect a physician to know his or her own limitations and not go beyond them, to seek outside counsel, to protect me from himself as well as from myself.

4. I expect a physician to make a difference for good in my life.

And when I am a follower, I expect the same from a leader:

1. I expect leaders to take the initiative in diagnosing and prescribing. They must figure out what the church or organization needs and how to meet those needs. Of course I want someone who will ask questions and listen wisely. But I don't want a leader who only seeks to implement the inclinations of the group.

2. I expect leaders to do what is in the best interest of those who follow. They dare not give primary concern to their salary, their position, their career, or meeting their own needs through others. They must be motivated by the best interests of their followers.

3. I expect leaders to know their limitations. If they are not capable of solving the problems, recruiting the personnel, managing the resources, then they will bring in the help and counsel of those who do know.

4. I expect leaders to make a difference for good in the church or organization.

Peter Drucker says that there is no correlation between potential and performance. There are lots of people who have had great potential but have never done anything with it. What counts is performance. Great leaders are those who *do* something.

This is not to say that leaders do not fail. They probably fail more often and on a larger scale than the average person. Winston Churchill finished secondary school at the bottom of his class. He considered himself a failure as First Lord of the Admiralty in World War I. But he failed because he was willing to be a leader who led and took risks. His followers recognized this and called him back to leadership in Britain's greatest hour of need.

Leaders are active, not passive people. They initiate. They do. They risk. As we face the exciting changes at the end of this century and the beginning of the next, we are like those rival basketball teams. Poised on the brink, waiting for the buzzer, who will grab the ball of change and make the throw?

Chapter 14

Time to Decide

EAVESDROP ON most important committee meetings and you'll hear a major mistake that regularly causes problems for churches and para-church organizations. Individuals make the same mistake. So do many businesses. The mistake is deciding what to do.

Search committees can be the worst offenders. Before the first meeting even begins, someone suggests a name. Then the discussion rolls out, with conversation galore on the suitability of the proposed candidate. I've sat in meetings where the chairman proposed that no specific names be considered until the fifth meeting, only to have a member (or even the same chairman) suggest a name immediately after the committee had agreed not to suggest any names at that point.

We are like sixth graders doing arithmetic homework; we want to go right to the answer without working through the problem. We want to get right to the exciting part—the important part. Except that working the problem is necessary if we are to get the correct answer. The process of reaching the decision is as important as the decision itself. It is, in fact, a vital part of decision-making.

So whether corporately or individually, in the church or the para-church, planned changes should come through a multiple-step process.

#1—Define the Issue

What is the problem? What is the real issue? Can it be summarized in a single sentence? Does everyone agree on what the issue is?

Defining the issue may be very hard work. Writing it down takes discipline. Getting agreement takes time. But without such definition and agreement a good decision is unlikely, and successful implementation may be impossible.

Take the example of Community Church, which formed a committee to propose plans for construction of a new auditorium for worship services. As happens in most committees, someone suggested the solution at the first meeting: "Let's build a 5,000-square-foot room with moveable seating so it can serve as a multi-purpose space that we can use to attract more young people for weekday events." That sounded fine until an older committee member said, "I don't feel like I've gone to church unless there are fixed pews. We're supposed to build a sanctuary to worship God, not a recreation room to entertain teenagers." The debate had begun, and agreement was difficult, if not impossible, because no one had really defined the problem.

Perhaps the real issue was not a building at all. Community Church served a community of longtime members who no longer lived in the neighborhood. Building construction was an attempt to rejuvenate a declining church. But why was it declining? Why did newcomers seldom stay for more than a couple of months? Why were there so many short tenure pastors who left unhappy? Could there be something wrong in the "body" that a new building wouldn't fix?

Answering such questions is far more work and may even be far more expensive than designing a 5,000-square-foot addition. For Community Church it took weeks of work to define the issue, but it was well worth it:

Community Church needs a new purpose and vision in order to serve God in the future as in the past. This will require a major evaluation of our entire ministry and a probable reorganization to effectively minister to people on the outside while continuing to minister to those who are already members.

It took fourteen months for Community Church to work through a process that adequately addressed the problem. All the results aren't in yet, but we do know that the suggested building was never built. Instead, the church sold their facilities and relocated to a warehouse while a new building was constructed. Some of the money from selling the old site went into additional staff and programs, and for the first time in years there is new excitement about the church's programs and potential.

The cost has been high: several older families left the church when the old building was sold; a once debt-free congregation now owes $675,000 to the bank; and the warehouse isn't as comfortable as the old downtown building. Some think the price was too high. Most think they got a bargain.

What Community Church did is what we all can do. The principle applies to calling a pastor, evangelizing a community, buying a bus, or changing careers. Instead of jumping to a conclusion, start at the beginning and define the real issue. Doing so forces us to answer "Why?" and define what we consider to be success.

For one, success may be reaching large numbers of non-Christians for Jesus Christ. For another, success is remaining faithful no matter what. I believe that success for both Christians and for Christian organizations is doing what God wants done and doing it well—the very best we can. The actual implementation of such success varies widely with time and place. Sometimes success will be numerical growth by the thousands; at other times success will mean dying as martyrs until the last believer in the town is dead. Success for one church will require sticking with the denomination as a witness, while for another church of the same denomination it will require disaffiliation as an example.

No fixed formulas work everywhere. Serving God is different from one time and place to another. It requires revelation, relevance, prayer, wisdom, and time. And once we have defined our issue and determined our measurement of success, let us be slow to criticize others who come to different conclusions regarding their own situations. Since our only final authority for faith and practice is the Bible, we must strive to be as broad as it is broad and as narrow as it is narrow. I find the Bible to be very narrow in the call to follow Jesus Christ and surprisingly broad in the acceptable ways of living out our positive answer to Christ's call.

#2—Get the Facts

Once the problem is defined, the next step in the decision process is assembling the facts so that we can be as objective as possible. It is rarely possible to get all the data to guarantee 100% accuracy; it takes too long, and some information is just not available. Like the members of a jury, we must learn what we can in order to make our best decision "beyond a reasonable doubt."

The nature of the facts we need to get depends on the issue defined. When calling a pastor, facts focus on the candidates' suitability, experience, and availability. When buying a building, the facts deal with location, price, access, zoning, and design.

Usually the fact-finding step begins with a list of research assignments. Doing those assignments often leads to a longer list because we discover how little we knew at the start. This step continues until enough data has been gathered to underpin a comfortable decision with predictability of success.

When Wooddale Church determined that the issue was "how to become an outreaching church," the factual research focused on the people we hoped to reach for Jesus Christ. We made door-to-door visits asking people about their needs. We hired a research firm to conduct a scientific poll of persons within a five-mile radius in order to learn about them. We studied census data. These and other methods enabled us to better understand our non-Christian and unchurched neighbors.

One of the most interesting research efforts employed focus groups. Through a research company we recruited a dozen unchurched men and women aged 25–50 for each group, and they were each paid $20 for the 90-minute sessions, during which a facilitator asked questions and sought their responses to various documents. The study team from the church observed from a different room through a one-way mirror.

When asked why they didn't go to church, the number one reason they gave was "Churches are always asking for your money." When showed the church ads from the Minneapolis newspaper, they had two primary responses: (1) they were unfamiliar with these ads, indicating that they rarely or never read them; (2) they laughed at many of the ads or found them difficult to read and understand.

The facilitator passed out pictures of people and asked the group to identify their denominations. At first there was high resistance to the notion that denomination could be determined by appearance. Then a man held up one of the pictures and said, "I can tell you one thing. This guy isn't a Mormon." The man in the picture was black. Then a woman held up a picture and said, "This woman is a Baptist!" Everyone in the focus group agreed. The woman in the picture was attractive, about 50 years old, seated in a living room chair with a book on the table beside her and a cat curled up on the floor. When the facilitator asked how they knew this person was a Baptist, the woman said, "She's perfect, and all Baptists think they are perfect!"

The focus groups were only one part of getting the facts, but they did help us understand and face three realities about reaching the unchurched in suburban Minneapolis: (1) minimize money talk; (2) church page ads don't reach the unchurched; (3) "Baptist" is not a positive word for some unchurched people.

Good decisions depend on accumulating information. Getting the facts is a lot of hard work, but well worth it.

#3—Consider the Alternatives

Through the process of defining the issue and getting the facts, alternatives will naturally appear. Those alternatives should be recorded along the way so that they can be considered during the decision-making process. For a search committee, alternatives may be the available candidates. For setting a purpose, alternatives may range from evangelizing to educating. One alternative for some distressed churches and organizations is closing down. On the personal level, alternatives may include anything from recommitment to resignation.

Typically, new alternatives trigger new research, and new research triggers new alternatives. Theoretically the process could go on forever, so it may be necessary to set a deadline beyond which no further research or alternatives will be accepted, unless the reasons for extension are unusually strong.

When the alternatives are weighed, spiritual and ethical issues are very important. While prayer for wisdom and divine direction is necessary all along the way, it is crucial at this stage.

Alternatives must also be tested against the Bible. For example, when we were deciding about changing the name of the church, someone on the committee was assigned to research the New Testament. No biblical defense or precedent for denominational church names was found, nor does the Bible set any rules for local church names. Therefore we concluded that the name of the church may be culturally determined. It was a somewhat more difficult decision when considering a Saturday night worship service. Study of the New Testament led to the conclusion that Sunday ("the Lord's Day") is normative for Christian worship but not required.

In some cases there may be nonnegotiables that are extrabiblical. For example, a denominational seminary requires professors to be members of one of that denomination's churches. This stipulation is not a biblical requirement, but the seminary administrators are bound by the denominational rules and must consider this nonnegotiable when recruiting new faculty members.

Often parishioners moving to another part of the country ask me how to select a new church home. My advice usually boils down to two recommendations: (1) select a church where the Bible is taught and lived; (2) select a church where you are comfortable. It's all part of considering the alternatives.

Another part of the consideration is anticipating the effects of each alternative. In extreme cases a proposed alternative may have much to recommend it, but the cost will be schism in the church and possible destruction of the organization. Such a high price may be required if the issue is the truth of Christianity or the sexual morality of top leadership—but rarely should people be divided or ministries destroyed over minor matters.

Most important is that a clear understanding of the Bible, ethics, effects, and research be applied to every alternative proposed. This will reduce the number of alternatives to only a few. Or sometimes all the alternatives will be eliminated and new alternatives must be initiated. In every case the alternatives should be tested against the standards of Scripture, principles of morality, requirements of the organization, cost, and data collected. Then it is time to decide.

#4—Make the Decision

This is what everyone has been waiting for—making the actual decision: changing the purpose; choosing the leader; buying the building; revising the rules; expanding the enterprise; closing the doors. Despite everyone's eagerness to reach this point, however, deciding can be very difficult.

Who should decide? The majority, since we operate democratically? God, since we operate theocratically? The people who did the research, since they know best? The people who will implement the decision, since they are responsible? Those most affected by the decision, since they have the most to gain or lose?

There is truth and merit in each of these responses, and it

is good to involve as many as possible in ownership of important decisions. But there is a better answer to the question "Who should decide?" The decision should be made by those who are best qualified to make the decision. This seems so obvious and simple—yet it is a principle that is seldom followed.

Search committees are the most flagrant examples of failure to follow this simple principle. Search committees are too often chosen to be representative rather than competent. A six-member committee must have a quota of males and females, rich and poor, young and old, majority and minority, or whatever the various factions might be. Except these may not be the wisest persons available. It is far better to choose those who pray fervently, think clearly, work hard, and make wise decisions.

If they are given authority by the body, the best-qualified persons will be the ones most likely to make good decisions that will be accepted by the organization.

An essential part of making the decision is deciding. Again, this may seem overly simple, but the issue here is the matter of not prolonging the process until the decision is too late. Delay may be motivated by fear of making an obvious but unpopular decision (like firing the pastor or closing the church) or by an overzealous attempt to get all the answers in advance. There is never enough time to gather *all* data, consider *all* alternatives, and make *perfect* decisions. Christian stewardship requires the best use of available resources, not perfection. A good decision reflects both stewardship and faith, trusting God for the final outcome.

When the decision to change has been made, it should be communicated throughout the organization to those affected by it. This requires frequent, redundant communications. Those to whom the ideas are new need sufficient time to process the proposed change. Most people need to hear, consider, react, interact, and accept before they buy into the change. It is not only unfair to expect others to agree in an hour to a decision that took a year, but it often results in initial rejection. Acceptance of new ideas takes time.

As others in the organization process the proposed change, they may come up with questions and ideas not previously considered. Leaders who listen, reconsider, and remain open to new ideas are most likely to see the essence of proposed changes implemented.

#5—Do It!

Implementation is the final, critical step in the process of decision and change. Recognizing that some members will not own a decision until they actually participate in it means that there should be minimum delay between deciding and doing. Don't wait for everyone to agree.

The leaders who decided are wise to participate in implementation, but it is also crucial to involve persons most affected. For example, if the change involves a move, have the employees help set up the furniture in the new office. Those who didn't want to move will begin to grow more comfortable with the change if they help hang the pictures and place the photocopiers.

Obviously large changes are harder to accept and implement than smaller changes. Breaking the larger whole into smaller parts is often the most practical secret to making changes happen. One midwestern church made the difficult decision to relocate from an inner city site to a suburban site, and the decision polarized the membership. Wise leaders divided up the process into smaller steps. First they held a Bible study in the suburbs; then they offered worship services in both locations with the same pastor. After a couple of years the board offered to have a church continue meeting at the old site, but everyone opted to move to the suburb and the old building was sold.

With action comes failure. It is often part of success. Failures legitimately call the organization back to reconsidering but not to rescinding the decision. Such reconsidering often strengthens the original decision.

Transitions

"Making Sense of Life's Changes" is the subtitle of William Bridges's book *Transitions*. Bridges was an English professor who underwent a career change. During the process he led a support group of other people who were also in major life transitions. From their experiences and other research, Bridges concluded that every significant change has three essential stages: Endings; The Neutral Zone; and The New Beginning.

Endings are the beginning of change. Often this requires a grief process that takes us through the steps from denial to resistance to acceptance. Perhaps the most painful part of ending is the sense of finality. We have become so comfortable with the old way that it is almost impossible to imagine a new way.

In extreme cases it can even be difficult to cope with the ending of bad things. The prisoner who has lived in the penitentiary for most of his life is frightened at the prospect of leaving the security and familiarity of his cell and facing the challenges of the outside world.

Even positive endings can be difficult. Parents who celebrate a child's graduation from high school or college know that a major chapter of life has ended, never to return.

The Neutral Zone is a period of reorientation, an "in between time" that is often unstable and uncertain. We feel disconnected. We have neither the comfortable familiarity of the old nor the fresh assurance of the new. The neutral zone is most obvious when someone is in between jobs; when a spouse has died and the widowed mate has not yet established a single life or remarried; or when a person has retired but has not yet developed a retirement lifestyle.

This neutral zone is particularly important in organizations. The founder has retired or died. The great days are all yesterday. The new leader just doesn't measure up yet. Everyone begins to wonder if there is any future at all. It can be a painful and tense time. However, when rightly understood, the neutral zone becomes positive—an opportunity to celebrate and grieve the past without rushing into permanent commitments for the future. This is when new ideas can be considered and new directions explored. Compare the neutral zone to the hibernation of winter between the seasons of green and growth.

The New Beginning is when hope is rekindled and new chapters are written in earnest. There is either a renewal of original purpose or the establishment of new purpose. Fresh starts do not negate the past; they simply accept the reality and the opportunity of change.

In churches the new beginning devotes today's energy to meet today's challenges and minister to today's generation. It means building on the past, but not trying to relive the past. It is the signal that change is complete.

Most people and organizations make it through all three stages of the transitions to change. Some do it smoothly; for others it means tremendous upheaval. It's probably never easy for anyone. What is important is understanding the inevitability of change, seeing change as a process that takes time, and working one's way through the stages.

A Final Word

In recent years the hurricane forces of change have dramatically altered our societal landscape. The changes are breathtaking, and some skeptics wonder if the church and Christianity can survive.

Let there be no doubt—the cause and church of Jesus Christ will not only survive but will thrive!

Jesus was and is the greatest change agent in the universe. The Incarnation was and is the greatest union of revelation and relevance ("The Word became flesh and made his dwelling among us," John 1:14). Jesus changes sinners into saints—the ultimate human transformation. He then forms those saints into the church, "and the gates of Hades will not overcome it" (Matt. 6:18).

The church of Jesus Christ could not be destroyed by Roman edict or Communist cruelty. It flourished under both. Christ's church is extraordinary—changing with every generation yet keeping the Gospel truth unchanged. No other institution comes close; nothing compares to it. And all because Jesus Christ is God, the church is supernatural, and the outcome is divinely determined.

As the twentieth century ends and the twenty-first century begins, Christians are privileged to see God perform His great acts through Christ's church one more time. Perhaps the best time of all!